Charting
made simple

A beginner's guide to charting success

Charting
made simple

Roger Kinsky

Wrightbooks

First published 2011 by Wrightbooks
an imprint of John Wiley & Sons Australia, Ltd
42 McDougall Street, Milton Qld 4064

Office also in Melbourne

Typeset in 11/13.4 pt Berkeley

© Roger Kinsky 2011

The moral rights of the author have been asserted

National Library of Australia Cataloguing-in-Publication data:

Author:	Kinsky, Roger.
Title:	Charting made simple: a beginner's guide to charting success / Roger Kinsky.
ISBN:	9780730375760 (pbk.)
Notes:	Includes index.
Subjects:	Investment analysis. Stocks.
Dewey Number:	332.642

Printed in China by Printplus Limited

Cover design by Peter Reardon, Pipeline Design <www.pipelinedesign.com.au>

10 9 8 7 6 5 4 3 2 1

Disclaimer

Contents

Preface

Following on from the positive reception by readers of my book *Shares Made Simple*, my publisher and I decided that the 'made simple' paradigm could ideally be applied to charting (or technical analysis). Technical analysis can be an elusive and often difficult-to-understand method shrouded in a certain amount of mystique that deters many would-be traders or investors from using it. That's a great pity, as technical analysis can improve profitability when used on its own or in conjunction with fundamental analysis by both longer term investors and shorter term traders.

My aim is to explain the most important aspects of technical analysis in the simplest possible way, so as to make the book easy to understand for those who hitherto have only tinkered with the method or avoided it altogether. Although the book is aimed primarily at beginners, I trust that more experienced readers may obtain some new insights of value to them.

The book contains many solved examples to highlight the principles. To allow readers to practise their skills and reinforce understanding some examples are in the form of self-test exercises where my interpretation is given in the appendix rather than in the body of the chapter. There's an element of subjectivity in technical analysis that's an inherent part of the method so interpretations can vary and there is no single correct solution. I've included many tips and suggestions, but please remember that they're my personal preferences and they mightn't always be appropriate for you so you need to use your own discretion. In addition, bear in mind that because technical analysis is not an exact science, tools and indicators don't always give reliable outcomes and even with the best interpretation not all your trades will be profitable. The aim is to improve the likelihood of success and maximise your overall trading profitability.

There are well over 50 different charting tools and indicators available, so clearly I had to decide which to include and which to exclude. Because CommSec is by far the most widely used online trading site in Australia, I decided to include all the tools and indicators available on this site, with the exception of the stochastic indicator. I excluded this indicator as I feel it's a rather advanced tool suitable for an experienced technical analyst and not really appropriate in an introductory text. In some cases I've included some tools or indicators not available on the CommSec site when I think these are important and worth including.

Every effort has been made to ensure the book is free of errors but in the real world perfection is difficult to achieve. I welcome feedback from readers who may have any constructive comments or suggestions for improvement. Please email me at <rkinsky@bigpond.com> or <rkinsky1@bigpond.com> or contact John Wiley & Sons, who will forward any correspondence to me. I will promptly reply to any emails or letters I receive.

Finally, I'd like to wish you every success when using technical analysis with your share investing or trading, and I trust that this book will assist you in achieving good outcomes.

Roger Kinsky
Woollamia, NSW
January 2011

Acknowledgements

I would like to thank CommSec and Incredible Charts for giving permission to reproduce charts and web pages included as examples in this book.

chapter 1

Introducing technical analysis

In this chapter I'll describe technical analysis and outline its purpose and the reasons why you should use it, as well as the limitations of the method. I'll also show you how to calculate profitability and how you can set yourself up so you can start using technical analysis. In later chapters I'll describe in more detail technical analysis tools and techniques you can consider using.

Technical analysis

Technical analysis is the analysis of trade prices to detect historical trends and trend changes to allow you to predict the most likely future scenario. The best way to analyse price action is with a chart, so technical analysis is also known as charting.

The purpose of technical analysis

Historical analysis is interesting, but is of little use unless you can use the analysis to look forward as well. Of course no-one can predict the future, but your aim in using technical analysis is to forecast the most likely (or probable) future price moves and to identify the best times to buy or sell. You're not dealing with certainty or aiming for infallibility; rather you're trying to swing the probabilities in your favour. That's to say, the fundamental purpose of technical analysis is to give you a trading edge allowing you to maximise trading profits and minimise losses.

Tip

Studying technical analysis is good mental gymnastics to keep your mind active, but there's little point to it unless your endeavours allow you to predict the most probable future price action and help you to identify times when you should buy or sell.

Technical analysis tools

There are many tools you can use to help you analyse charts and form your conclusions. Tools that provide indications are known naturally enough as indicators. The most valuable indicators are primary ones, but you can also use secondary indicators—known as filters—to refine the primary indications. Indicators can provide trading signals, which are significant markers that you can use for trading purposes; that is, to indicate a good time to trade.

Various mathematical formulas and procedures—known as algorithms—are used to calculate an indicator. Like prices, indicators are presented in chart form, and indicator trends can provide trading signals when viewed in conjunction with price trends.

If you understand how an indicator is calculated it will help you to interpret the indicator. If you're not mathematically inclined, don't despair. I'll do my best to explain how each indicator is derived as simply as possible, but you don't really need to understand the mathematical procedures to use an indicator. It's rather like using a prescription medicine—while it's good to know the ingredients and how it's made, that's not vital. What you really want to know is its purpose, how to use the medicine properly and the benefits and risks associated with it. In the same way you can use technical analysis tools and indicators without fully understanding the mathematical calculations, provided you understand the purpose of each one, how to use it and its benefits and limitations.

Tip

To use technical analysis tools and indicators to best advantage you need to know the purpose of each one, how to use it and its benefits and limitations. If you can also understand how each one is derived, so much the better.

Understanding technical analysis

Some investors regard technical analysis as being of little value or too complex and hard to understand, and therefore disregard it. Others subscribe to some whiz-bang proprietary program that's claimed to make a fortune for those who use it. There are many websites and specialist programs that cater for this market and require users to subscribe and pay to access the charts and analysis algorithms.

My aim is to demystify the complexity and to provide you with the knowledge and skills that will enable you to use a sound technical analysis system that will guide you in making good trading decisions without relying on a user-pays system. I'll show you how to obtain charts and technical analysis tools that are available to all from websites that don't charge their users a fee.

Most chapters include worked examples to assist your understanding, as well as some where I haven't provided my interpretation in the chapter but in the appendix. This will enable you to try your hand at technical analysis without distraction and then compare your interpretation with mine. Each chapter concludes with a summary of the main points.

Tip

You can understand and use technical analysis without relying on the expertise of others or subscribing to a user-pays system.

Technical analysis versus fundamental analysis

Technical analysis is very different to another important method of investment analysis known as fundamental analysis. Fundamental analysis considers factors such as products and markets of a business, the length of time it's been in operation, its size and market capitalisation, as well as financial statistics including profitability (earnings), dividends, assets and liabilities. The basic principle underpinning fundamental analysis is that businesses with sound fundamentals should prove to be good investments in the long run. Fundamental analysis is primarily used by investors who want to identify sound longer term investments.

On the other hand, technical analysis isn't the least bit concerned with fundamentals, and indeed you don't even have to know anything about the business. The only important consideration driving technical analysis is price action. While the three P's of property investment are position, position, position, the three P's of technical analysis are price, price, price.

Tip

The three P's of technical analysis are price, price, price.

Time frame of an investment

The value of fundamental and technical analysis is related to the planned time frame of an investment, as shown in figure 1.1.

Figure 1.1: relationship between fundamental and technical analysis and time frame

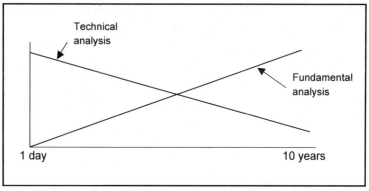

This diagram shows that as the time frame increases, the importance of technical analysis decreases while the importance of fundamental analysis increases. Technical analysis is most valuable in the short term but loses relevance as the time frame increases because price action is dynamic and ever-changing and this makes long-term price predictions too uncertain to be useful. On the other hand, businesses with sound fundamentals might experience short-term setbacks but in the longer term should recover and prosper and conform to expectations.

Tip

Technical analysis is most valuable in the shorter term, whereas fundamental analysis is most valuable in the longer term.

Technical analysis and market sentiment

Technical analysis uses mathematical algorithms to identify and predict price moves; nevertheless, the most important factor driving prices is market sentiment. Market sentiment is the consensus opinion of those trading the market.

Consequently, another way of looking at technical analysis is to view it as a tool that aims to detect traders' sentiment and changes in sentiment. These sentiments apply to a single business entity or to the market as a whole. They include:

⇨ *optimism:* a positive outlook based on the opinion that all's well and prices will rise. Optimistic traders want to buy and are known as bulls. If there's enough of them to drive most prices higher, the market as a whole will rise and is known as a bull market

⇨ *pessimism:* a negative outlook based on the opinion that all's not well and prices will fall. Pessimistic traders are looking for the exit (want to sell) and are known as bears. If there's enough of them to drive most prices lower, the market as a whole will fall and is known as a bear market

⇨ *profit desire:* sometimes referred to as 'greed', but I don't like this description as it implies excessive desire for profit. In my view all traders have a right to make as much profit as they can; after all, they're risking their money and using their wits in the process, so the better they are at it, the more profit they're entitled to make

⇨ *loss avoidance:* also referred to as 'fear' of loss, but again I don't like this description and prefer to think of this sentiment as the desire to avoid a loss or protect profits and cash them in before they could evaporate or turn into losses. Interestingly, psychological experiments indicate that most people's motivation is more influenced by the desire to protect what they have rather than the desire to make more profit.

The sentiments of optimism and pessimism, profit desire and loss avoidance are conflicting ones, and the way prices move depends on the dominant sentiment at the time. This in turn can be influenced by a whole host of factors, including—believe it or not—the weather! It's also the case that traders influence one another, and a move by a few traders can gather pace and accelerate as other traders join in. This effect is known as momentum, and it can cause prices to reach irrational levels—either overbought or oversold. I'll discuss this important phenomenon in greater detail in later chapters.

Tip

Technical analysis can't analyse human sentiments but it can analyse market action and infer how sentiments are changing.

How reliable is technical analysis?

Technical analysts can give the impression that the method can be used by anyone to make a trading fortune provided that the necessary knowledge and skills are acquired and applied correctly. It follows that if you use the method unsuccessfully it's your fault: you didn't have the necessary skills or knowledge. In reality, no charting tool or indicator is foolproof; that is, none are 100% reliable. No matter how well you understand or apply a tool or indicator you won't win all the time. All tools and indicators can give good signals in some situations but not in all, because markets have an element of unpredictability that's an inherent part of the process.

Inherent unpredictability in market price movements doesn't mean technical analysis should be disregarded. I liken technical analysis to weather forecasting because there's also an inherent unpredictability in the weather. Many factors can affect it, and small and unknown changes can build up and multiply in chaotic and essentially unpredictable ways. But that doesn't mean that because weather forecasting isn't an exact science we should disregard it. The forecasts mightn't always be right but they're more often right than wrong. Nowadays it would be foolish to ignore weather forecasts when planning any activity where the weather could affect the outcome.

Tip

No technical analysis tool or indicator is foolproof, and you shouldn't adopt the mindset that there's a fully reliable system or method to use if only you can discover it. Don't be discouraged when your trades aren't always profitable—some losing trades are inevitable.

Trading instruments

Trading instrument is the general term used to describe something of value (an asset) that's tradeable; that is, there's a free market with willing buyers and sellers for it. Some trading instruments are physical commodities such as sugar, corn and oil, whereas others are financial assets such as shares or currency (forex—foreign exchange). Other types of trading instruments are derivatives (or synthetic instruments); the instrument itself doesn't have any actual physical presence but is a financial creation that's based on the underlying asset of value. Derivatives include rights, options, warrants, CFDs (contracts for difference) and index futures (contracts where the underlying asset is a share price index). In these cases the buyer (or taker) of the instrument doesn't actually own the asset but enters into a contract to buy or sell it at a certain price at some time in the future.

The principles of technical analysis are applicable to any trading instrument where there's historical price information available, but in this book I'll consider ordinary Australian shares only. If you're interested in trading other instruments the principles apply in the same way but you'll need to investigate the special trading conditions involved.

Tip

Technical analysis can be applied to any tradeable instrument where prices are determined by free market competition between buyers and sellers. However, trading conditions and contracts vary between the different instruments.

Trading terminology

Trading is a general term used to mean either buying or selling an instrument. A completed trade is known as a transaction. With shares and most assets that have a physical presence there are only two sides to the coin: you either buy or sell. Of course you can also hold, and this term is used to mean that you take no action; you don't buy or sell but if you've already bought you continue with your current shareholding.

With some of the more sophisticated trading instruments other types of trades and terminology are used. These include:

⇨ *go long:* buy, or hold what you've bought

⇨ *go short (shorting):* sell, or reduce your exposure

⇨ *open a position:* take up one side of a contract

⇨ *close a position:* take up the opposite side of the original contract

⇨ *write:* create a contract

⇨ *take:* become a party to a contract by conforming to the terms and conditions that apply.

Because I'm concentrating on ordinary shares in this book I'll use the terms 'buy' and 'sell' to denote the two basic types of trades involved with shares.

Profiting in bull and bear markets

Trading profits derive from capital gains which are obtained by selling at a higher price than the original purchase price (including transaction and holding costs). This principle applies to all trading instruments. Most profits are made in bull markets (when prices are rising), and in this case the buy transaction comes before the sell transaction: you buy first and sell later.

It's also possible to make profits in a bear market—that is, when the price is falling—by short selling shares or by trading options, warrants or CFDs. For example, you can buy put options, write call options or short sell. Short selling is a special type of trade where the sell transaction comes before the buy transaction: you sell first and buy later. In this transaction you can profit from falling prices because you buy back later at a lower price than your original selling price. Short selling of ordinary shares in Australia is tightly regulated by the Australian Securities & Investments Commission (ASIC), and is a facility provided by only a restricted number of brokers. CommSec (Australia's largest online share broker) doesn't have the facility. Short selling with CFDs is straightforward, and this is one reason why some traders prefer to trade CFDs rather than shares.

Tip

If you're interested in learning more about trading the more sophisticated instruments, a good place to start is my book Online Investing on the Australian Sharemarket *as it contains more information about this type of trading.*

Trading versus investing

An investor is primarily concerned with medium- to long-term profitability. Short-term price movements are of little interest and are regarded as ripples caused by changes in day-to-day buying and selling sentiment. Share investors want to buy and hold sound businesses that have a proven track record and good fundamentals, so they use fundamental analysis to identify these businesses. Investors profit over the term of the investment by receiving dividends and from capital gains if eventually they decide to sell. Because investors don't need to trade frequently, they don't need to follow the market closely. Indeed, some employ a 'bottom drawer' approach by buying and then holding and paying little attention to market movements. They consider selling only if some dramatic adverse change has taken place.

Share traders are interested in price movements and market sentiment only and aim to make short-term profits by trading. Dividends aren't a consideration for traders and profits primarily derive from capital gains (a trader will of course profit from a dividend if it is paid while the shares are held). The underlying value of the shares is of no concern to a trader, who isn't interested in fundamentals. Therefore traders rely principally on technical analysis and ignore fundamental analysis. They often trade speculative or risky shares that would be avoided by an investor. Indeed, from an experienced short-term trader's viewpoint, the more risky the better—can you see why? The reason is that speculative and risky shares are volatile; that is, there are large short-term movements in price. Short-term traders can use these price changes to make quick trading profits. Always keep in mind though that the higher the volatility the higher the risk, so you can also make quick losses.

Nowadays computers process share trades, and because computers operate so rapidly trading time frames can be very short—as little as one or two seconds, or even fractions of a second. Naturally, price changes in such a short time period will usually be small—perhaps fractions of a cent—but because large sums of money (parcel values) can be involved the profit can still be substantial if trading costs are low.

Short-term traders need to follow the market closely; if not continuously, at least by checking prices on a frequent basis each day. Some are day traders; that is, they buy and sell in the course of a day's trading. Day traders are usually reluctant to hold open positions overnight and will try to close out all open positions before the market closes each day.

The distinction between share investing and trading is summarised in table 1.1 (overleaf).

Table 1.1: share investing versus trading

	Investing	Trading
Time frame	Medium to long	Short
Source of profit	Dividends and capital gains	Primarily capital gains
Monitoring frequency	Weekly to monthly	Very often (possibly continuously)
Investment instrument	Good-quality shares	All listed shares and share derivatives

Investor/traders and trader/investors

While there's a distinction between investing and trading, it doesn't necessarily follow that everyone who buys and sells is either an investor or a trader. Many investors can be regarded as investor/traders because they trade with some of their investing capital. For example, they might invest 80% of their capital and trade with 20% of it. On the other hand, many traders may also invest some of their capital over the medium to long term and they could be regarded as trader/investors.

Tip

If you're a long-term investor and you have the time and inclination, it's possible to improve your profitability through short-term trading with some of your capital.

Should an investor use technical analysis?

From what you've read so far perhaps you've formed the impression that if you're investing for the longer term you should use fundamental analysis and if you're trading in the shorter term you should use technical analysis. But that's too simplistic, and I believe that investors as well as traders can use technical analysis to improve profitability. Fundamental analysis is a valuable tool for identifying sound shares for investment, but technical analysis can identify market sentiment and the best time to buy (or sell) those shares. It's counterproductive to buy good-quality shares as an investment if you buy them at the wrong time; for example, when the price is falling. In addition, technical analysis is very useful for investors when monitoring price performance of shares in their portfolio.

Tip

Investors as well as traders can use technical analysis to improve profitability.

When to use technical analysis

There are three different times when you should consider using technical analysis:

⇨ when monitoring and reviewing your share portfolio. Apart from keeping yourself up to date, the main purpose of monitoring and reviewing is to identify underperforming shares so you can decide whether to continue to hold or whether selling some (or all) of them is a better option. Technical analysis is an essential part of the monitoring and reviewing process as it highlights price trends and trend changes

⇨ to identify the best times to invest. You do this when you have some capital available and have identified shares you want to buy but you want to make sure you're buying them at the right time. You can also use technical analysis when you're considering selling and rebalancing your portfolio and you're investigating more attractive investing opportunities

⇨ for shorter term trading. Technical analysis is a vital aid when you're trying to make trading profits in a relatively short time frame as it allows you to identify price trend changes and opportunities for trading profits.

Tip

Technical analysis is a valuable method you can use when monitoring and reviewing or when identifying investing or trading opportunities.

Return on capital

When you make a trading profit the dollars involved aren't as significant as the return on capital; that is, the profit as a percentage of the capital you've outlaid. For example, if you make $200 profit on $1000 capital outlay that's significant as it represents a 20% return on capital. However, if the capital outlay is $10000 then the same $200 profit is a mere 2% return on capital — not enough to even keep up with inflation.

You also need to take into account the time frame (or term) involved. In my previous example $200 profit in one year for $1000 capital outlay is 20%, but if the profit accrued over 10 years then you're averaging only 2% per year. You can take into account the time frame by calculating an equivalent annual return. This enables you to compare apples with apples, because for a certain amount of profit, the shorter the term the higher the equivalent annual return.

I'll now show you how to calculate equivalent annual return. For the purpose of this calculation, I'll consider a trading year to consist of an average of 50 weeks with five trading days per week.

The trading profit formulas are:

⇨ Total cost = Buy price × Quantity + Trading cost

⇨ Total revenue = Selling price × Quantity − Trading cost

⇨ Profit = Total cost − Total revenue

⇨ Capital invested = (Total cost + Total revenue) ÷ 2

⇨ Return on capital = (Profit ÷ Capital invested) × 100

⇨ Equivalent annual return on capital (short-term investments) = Return on capital × 250 ÷ Elapsed days

⇨ Equivalent annual return on capital (medium-term investments) = Return on capital × 50 ÷ Elapsed weeks

Note:

⇨ The elapsed days or weeks is the number of trading days or weeks between the buy and sell transactions (opening and closing the contract).

⇨ I've assumed no holding costs are involved because that's the usual scenario with shares, unless you've taken out a margin loan or are trading CFDs.

⇨ The capital invested is the average capital invested.

⇨ If you make a loss rather than a profit, all formulas still apply but your revenue will be less than your cost and profit will be negative.

For long-term investments the above analysis is only approximate because of the effect of compounding.

You might want to consider setting up a spreadsheet to do the number crunching automatically. A more detailed explanation of the profit formulas and the concept of average capital invested are given in *Teach Yourself About Shares*.

Example

You buy a parcel of 5000 shares for $1.26 per share. You hold the shares for three weeks and three days and then sell them for $1.33. Your trading cost is $20 for each trade.

What is your equivalent annual return on capital?

Solution

Total cost = 1.26 × 5000 + 20 = $6320
Total revenue = 1.33 × 5000 − 20 = $6630
Profit = 6630 − 6320 = $310

Capital invested = (6320 + 6630) ÷ 2 = $6475
Return on capital = (310 ÷ 6475) × 100 = 4.79%
Elapsed days = 3 × 5 + 3 = 18
Equivalent annual return on capital = 4.79 × 250 ÷ 18
= **66.5%**

Conclusion

You can see that while the return on capital is a modest 4.79%, because the elapsed time between buying and selling is only 18 trading days the equivalent annual return is an impressive 66.5%.

Tip

You can make large profits from relatively small price changes if the elapsed time between the opening and closing trades is short.

Taxation considerations

Capital gains are taxable income, and tax payable on this income reduces your net profit. However, you can write gains off against losses, and if the time frame is 12 months or more only half the capital gain is taxable. For short-term trades this relief is of no benefit, but for longer term trades it's an important consideration. For example, if you've bought shares and held them for 10 or 11 months, it may well pay to keep them for a month or two more rather than sell, even though the price may fall in the intervening period. Of course, do your calculations carefully to decide which is the best option.

Tip

Teach Yourself About Shares contains more information about taxation considerations (for both capital gains and dividends), as well as formulas and worked examples that help you decide whether to sell or hold.

Stock codes

All Australian Securities Exchange–listed trading instruments are given an alphabetic identification code. For ordinary shares this code is a three-letter code; for example, Commonwealth Bank is CBA and Woolworths is WOW. For options, warrants, hybrids and so on, additional letters are added up to a total of six. Market and sector indices are also given an identification code; for example, the code for the All Ordinaries index is XAO and the Energy sector code is XEJ.

Share codes and index codes can be found on the Australian Securities Exchange (ASX) website. Also my books *Online Investing on the Australian Sharemarket* and *Teach Yourself About Shares* have a complete listing and description of market and sector codes.

Tip

It's a great time-saver to keep a list of the codes of interest to you in a conveniently accessible place.

Accessing technical analysis tools

The development of personal computers with fast and ready access to the internet has revolutionised technical analysis and given all investors and traders the opportunity to use technical analysis in the comfort and convenience of their own homes. Depending on the sophistication of the charting software it's often possible to customise a chart in various ways, including choosing the format and time period of the chart. In addition, you will be able to select and plot indicators from those available. In some cases you can also draw trendlines electronically on the chart and save your marked-up chart for future reference. A fascinating aspect is the speed at which your request is processed. Your requested charts appear on the screen almost instantaneously after you have made your selection and pressed the enter key.

To use technical analysis with any degree of sophistication you'll need a computer with an internet connection enabling you to access websites that provide share price charts and charting tools. Of course, you should use virus/Trojan checking software to reduce the risk of harmful infections.

Tip

It's a great advantage to use a large monitor for technical analysis because the larger the screen the easier it is to visually interpret charts.

Charting sites

There are essentially three different types of charting sites you can use:

⇨ online trading sites

⇨ free websites that provide a charting facility

⇨ subscription sites.

Online trading sites

If you trade online your trading website will most likely include a charting facility. In some cases (such as the Etrade site) the charting facility will be comprehensive and provide all the tools you require. In other cases, the charting software won't be sufficiently sophisticated and you may need to look elsewhere.

Tip

If you're contemplating a trade and you're using a website for technical analysis that's not the same as your online trading site, you can access both sites and toggle between them using the screen minimisation button.

Free-access websites

One of my principles (I call it the 'Kinsky Principle') is never to pay for anything that you can obtain for free. There are many websites you can access that provide a free charting facility, although some—such as the ASX site, <www.asx. com.au>—provide only very basic charts that aren't suitable for serious technical analysis. However, the ASX site is useful as a starting point for information about shares, particularly for company announcements.

There are excellent websites that provide sophisticated software with many charting tools available, but many are US websites that provide charts of US stocks only. In my opinion, the best free-access website in Australia that provides charts of all ASX-listed stocks is the Incredible Charts site, <www. incrediblecharts.com>, and it's one I usually use for technical analysis. In order to use this site you'll need to register and you'll be given a user ID number, but this is free. A similar site is the Big Charts site, <www.bigcharts.com>, but I prefer the Incredible Charts site. For other free sites please refer to my online investing book.

Tip

I suggest you register and explore the Incredible Charts site, regardless of what other charting software you use.

Subscription sites

Some chartists use a proprietary charting service. There's often a substantial upfront charge, and then there's also usually an ongoing monthly fee. The charting software provided is often part of a technical analysis package that includes a 'whiz bang' system that's claimed to produce superior results and enable subscribers to make big profits. I don't subscribe to any such packages and I don't believe that there's any one technical analysis system that will provide consistently superior returns. However, that's only a personal viewpoint and if you wish to subscribe to a system that you believe will do the job for you by all means give it a go. You can always opt out of the system at a later date if you aren't satisfied with the results. If you're interested I suggest you refer to my online investing book for site listings.

Some free-access sites (such as the Incredible Charts site) provide a basic charting facility free of charge but also provide a premium service that you can access by paying a fee. Again, I suggest you don't subscribe to a premium service unless you're convinced that you require more tools than are provided in the basic facility.

Tip

Don't subscribe to a user-pays charting service or technical analysis system unless you've explored the free options and you're convinced that you really need to pay for additional facilities. It isn't necessarily the case that the more expensive charting systems will produce more trading profits.

Choosing a broker

The more often you trade the more important it is to trade at low cost, particularly if you are trading relatively small parcel values. For example, a brokerage charge of $50 for a trade of $2000 amounts to $100 for a complete buy–sell transaction, and that's 5%. This high percentage fee considerably erodes your return on capital. However, if the brokerage is $20 a complete buy–sell transaction involves a fee of $40 and that's now a far more reasonable 2%.

Nowadays most traders trade online because of the low brokerage. There are approximately 20 online brokers operating in Australia, and they are often affiliated with major banks or financial institutions. The most popular online broker is CommSec (affiliated with the Commonwealth Bank).

CommSec has a relatively low fee structure and their charting facility provides a reasonable number of tools and indicators.

To use an online broker you'll need to register and provide ID and other details, including bank account authorisation for cash transfers with your nominated account. Once you register, you'll be given an account number and password to enable you to access the site and trade. An outstanding benefit of using an online broker is that once you register you can use all the technical analysis indicators and information available without the obligation to trade.

Tip

If you intend to trade on a regular basis use an online broker. Further details and comparisons of online brokers in Australia are given in my online investing book.

Chapter summary

⇨ Technical analysis is the historical analysis of prices to detect trends and trend changes to enable you to predict the most likely future price action.

⇨ Price action is best shown and analysed in chart form so the method is also known as charting.

⇨ Price action is a reflection of market sentiment. Technical analysis alerts you to changes in sentiment by inference from price trend changes. Sentiments that affect prices include optimism, pessimism, profit motive and loss avoidance. These sentiments play out in the market and dominance of one over others drives price movement.

⇨ Technical analysis uses indicators, which are tools that aid in the analysis of trends and trend changes.

⇨ No technical analysis indicator or system is 100% reliable. However, technical analysis can improve your likelihood of trading success.

⇨ Technical analysis differs from fundamental analysis in that it doesn't try to relate prices to any intrinsic or fair value.

⇨ Technical analysis can be applied to any trading instrument where historical price information is available.

⇨ Trading instruments can be commodities such as sugar or gold, shares, currencies or synthetic instruments (derivatives) such as options, index futures and CFDs.

⇨ Technical analysis is particularly useful for traders, who aim to make short-term profits from price movements. It is also of value to investors interested in medium- or long-term profitability as it facilitates timing of trades and the monitoring and reviewing process.

⇨ Trading profits derive from capital gains obtained when selling revenue is greater than purchase cost. Trading profits are usually made in bull markets by buying first and selling later. However, it's also possible to trade profitably in bear markets by short selling or by trading more sophisticated instruments.

⇨ The true measure of profitability is equivalent annual return on capital. This is the percentage return on capital on an equivalent annual basis.

⇨ Capital gains are considered as taxable income, but if shares are held for 12 months or more only half the gain is taxable.

⇨ Charts and indicators are best accessed on the internet. Many sites provide them, including free sites, online broking sites and subscription sites.

⇨ A most useful free site is the Incredible Charts site and it's well worthwhile registering and obtaining a user ID number so you can access the site whenever you want.

⇨ The best way of trading cheaply and rapidly is by using an online broker.

chapter 2

Charts

Charting is the backbone of technical analysis, and many types of charts are used. In this chapter I'll describe the charts that are commonly used and the advantages and limitations of each one.

Price charts

Because technical analysis is all about price action, the chart you'll most often want to look at is a price chart. In this type of chart price is shown on the y axis and time is shown on the x axis, as shown in figure 2.1 (overleaf).

Price scale

The price scale is usually linear; that is, the distance between each division is the same. For example, the distance between 1 and 2 is the same as the distance between 2 and 3, and so on. Another option is to use a logarithmic price scale, and in this scale the distance between 0.1 and 1 is the same as the distance between 1 and 10, and the same as the distance between 10 and 100.

The difference between a linear and logarithmic scale is shown in figure 2.2.

Figure 2.1: price chart axes

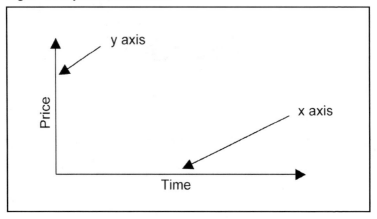

Figure 2.2: linear and logarithmic scales

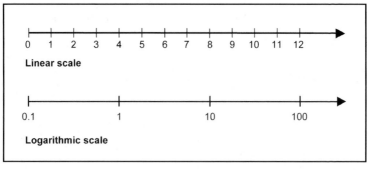

The logarithmic scale is less common than the linear scale but has an advantage compared to it. Consider a $1.00 price rise from $1.00 to $2.00, which is a return of 100% on capital invested. If the same $1.00 price rise is from $10.00 to $11.00, this gives a far lower return of 10%. On a linear scale price chart the $1.00 price increase looks the same in both cases, but not so on a logarithmic scale. On a logarithmic scale the same percentage change looks the same (not the same dollar value change), so a price change from $1.00 to $2.00 would appear much larger than a price change from $10.00 to $11.00. Indeed, the price would need to rise from $10.00 to $20.00 in order to look the same on a logarithmic scale because that's the same 100% increase.

Example 1

I've illustrated the difference between the two price scales with a hypothetical company—a long-term investor's dream company. The company is able to increase profits by 20% each year, so the earnings per share (EPS) increases by 20% each year. The market price of the shares increases from $1.00 by 20% each year, in step with the EPS. The price of the shares over an 11-year period is given in table 2.1.

Table 2.1: price increase each year

Year	1	2	3	4	5	6	7	8	9	10	11
Price	1.00	1.20	1.44	1.73	2.07	2.49	2.99	3.58	4.30	5.16	6.19

The price chart using both linear and logarithmic scales is illustrated in figure 2.3.

Figure 2.3: linear and logarithmic price charts

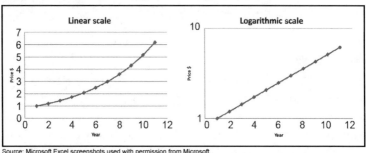

Source: Microsoft Excel screenshots used with permission from Microsoft.

You can see that the price appears as a curved line on a linear scale chart but a straight line on a logarithmic scale chart. An investor buying the shares and selling them later at any time during this 11-year period would make a capital gain of 20% per annum. The logarithmic scale chart indicates this because it's a straight line.

A downside to the logarithmic scale is that there aren't as many price gridlines, so it's more difficult to project across from the price line to read the price scale. Another problem is that many charting sites (such as the CommSec site) don't provide a logarithmic price scale (but the Incredible Charts site does).

If the price range isn't high in percentage terms there's not a significant difference in appearance between prices shown using the two scales. The logarithmic scale is most useful when there are large price changes, as might occur over a long time period. In my dream company example the price changed from $1.00 to over $6.00 in the 11-year time period charted, and that's over 600%. That's an uncommon scenario in most charts you'll look at because the time period will usually be shorter and the price is unlikely to change by more than 100%. Then there won't be a great deal of difference between prices shown on charts using the two scales.

Tip

If there's a large price range and charting software gives you the choice, you'll get a better impression of price trends if you use a logarithmic scale.

Price range

The price range is the variation from the highest to lowest prices that appear on the chart during the time period displayed. The charting software automatically adjusts the price scale according to the range, so the prices will conveniently fit in the available vertical space. Prices won't necessarily start at zero; for example, if the price varies from a low of $5.20 to a high of $5.80 in a given time frame, the chart might display prices from $5.00 to $6.00.

Time scale

In most price charts a linear scale is used for time, shown on the x axis. The distance between each time division is the same. In some charts a linear time scale isn't possible due to the nature of the chart. I'll explain these charts later.

Time period

With most charting software you'll be able to vary the time period over which the chart is drawn. Common periods are:

⇨ one day (intra-day) ⇨ eighteen months

⇨ one month ⇨ two years

⇨ three months ⇨ five years

⇨ six months ⇨ ten years

⇨ nine months ⇨ all data.

⇨ one year

In all charts (other than the intra-day chart), the extreme right side of the chart is updated to the close of trade for the previous trading period (day or week). The chart won't be updated in real time and won't show current price action. For example, if you're looking at a daily chart on Monday, the most recent price data shown will be last Friday's close.

The left-hand side of the chart (the starting point) depends on the time period you've chosen. For example, if the chart is a three-month chart the starting point will be three months back from the previous Friday if you're looking at the chart on Monday.

Tip

Many charting sites provide crosshairs that you can move across the chart. It's a most useful aid as it allows you to project across to the price axis or down to the time axis to read the values.

One day (intra-day) charts

A one-day or intra-day chart shows the price action as each trade takes place. Prices can change by a certain minimum amount — known as the tick — that depends on the price, so these charts are also known as tick charts. The chart starts by showing prices for the first trades of the day, then prices are plotted moving toward the right as trades occur. The amount of price action on the chart depends on the time at which you access the chart. If you access a chart at 11 am, you'll see only one hour's price action because the market opens at 10 am, whereas if you access the chart just before close at 4 pm you'll see almost all the price action for the day.

Tip

Not all sites provide intra-day charts (for example, they're not available on the Incredible Charts site). On sites that do have the facility (such as the CommSec site) there's a time delay (between 5 and 20 minutes) and it's a good idea to check this. If the chart doesn't automatically update you'll need to refresh the screen periodically to see the latest trades.

Example 2

An example of an intra-day chart is shown in figure 2.4. This chart from the CommSec site is for Tabcorp (TAH). The first trade took place at a price of $6.54, at 10.09 am, then the price quickly rose to $6.64, before falling back to $6.59 then rising again to $6.67 at 1.33 pm, which is the most recent data point. If I'd accessed the chart later in the day more trading data would be shown.

Trade volume is charted as a separate section below the price. I'll discuss volume later in this chapter and in greater detail in chapter 9.

The CommSec intra-day chart doesn't have the time scale marked, but when you access the chart on a computer you can see the time if you use the crosshairs tool.

Figure 2.4: intra-day chart

Source: www.CommSec.com.au

Tip

If you access an intra-day chart soon after market open-ing you won't see much action and it will be difficult to detect a trend.

Frequency

Frequency is the time division or time interval used on the time axis (x axis). Most charting software allows you to vary the frequency. The most common frequency is one day, and it's usually the default value. If you're accessing a chart over a long time period there'll be so many price data points that the chart may become difficult to interpret. There are about 250 trading days in a year, so if you're looking at a five-year chart with a frequency of one day there'll be about 1250 data points. In this case a weekly frequency will be more appropriate, and for really long time periods you might consider a monthly frequency.

Tip

Most of the chart examples in this book use a daily frequency because it's the frequency you'll most often use.

Choice of time period and frequency

Your choices of time period and frequency will depend on what's available in the charting software you're using and the extent to which you can customise. Generally speaking, the time period you select depends on the type of trade you're contemplating. For example, if you're thinking of long-term investing you'll want to look at a chart going back perhaps five or ten years, whereas if you're thinking of trading short term such a long time period won't be relevant. For short-term trading you'll most likely look at a three-month chart or perhaps a one-month chart, as well as an intra-day chart if you're thinking of trading that day.

If you're a longer term investor, I suggest the following time periods would be appropriate:

⇨ first, access a long-term chart, say five or ten years

⇨ next, look at a shorter term chart, say six months or so

⇨ finally, look at an intra-day chart on the day you're contemplating the trade.

You might question why you would want to look at an intra-day chart if you're a longer term investor. The reason I suggest this is that during the course of a day's trading prices can vary significantly, and the intra-day chart allows you to see the variation. For example, if you want to buy and the intra-day chart shows the price downtrending today, you might want to defer buying until later on in the day or wait to see what's happening tomorrow. On the other hand, if the price is uptrending and you want to sell, it might be best to defer placing the order.

Tip

When you want to place an order, an intra-day chart is worth looking at even if you're a longer term investor.

Volume

The volume of shares traded is important in technical analysis. It's the number of shares changing hands with each transaction, and because a share bought is also a share sold volume is the number of shares either bought or sold. So:

Volume = Number of shares traded = Number of shares bought = Number of shares sold

I'll discuss volume in detail in chapter 9, but for now I'll just point out that volume is customarily shown as a bar chart drawn below the price chart. For example, in figure 2.4 the volume chart is shown below the price chart. On the extreme right there's a number to give you an idea of the volume scale. In this chart the figure is 200k (200 000) and a line is drawn at this value. So you can see that on this day a relatively small number of shares were traded, except at around midday when 200 000 shares were traded at a price of about \$6.60. This is a parcel value of about \$1.32 million, so clearly this trade involved large investors or financial institutions. It's interesting to note that after this trade the price rose, and about an hour later the shares were trading at around \$6.67 — most likely because the large volume of trades previously soaked up all the available shares on offer and buyers needed to bid a higher price in order to get some shares.

Tip

Volume is an important consideration in technical analysis.

Types of price charts

There are many different types of price charts, of which the most common are:

⇨ line charts (and mountain charts)

⇨ OHLC charts

⇨ candle charts

⇨ equi-volume charts

⇨ percent charts

⇨ point and figure charts.

Line charts (and mountain charts)

In a line chart closing prices are connected by straight lines. For example, with a daily frequency chart closing prices each day are connected, and in a weekly chart closing prices at the end of each week (usually 4 pm Friday) are connected. A mountain chart is a line chart with a slight variation, in that the area below the line is lightly shaded and this makes interpretation a little easier.

Example 3

An example of a mountain chart is shown in figure 2.5. It's taken from the CommSec site and is for Commonwealth Bank (CBA) over a six-month period with frequency one day.

Figure 2.5: mountain chart

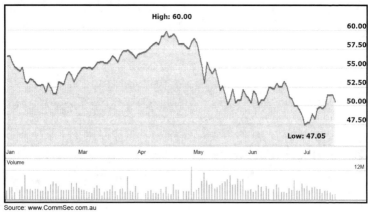

Source: www.CommSec.com.au

You can see from the volume that Commonwealth Bank shares have a high liquidity (high daily volume) and in one day during this period over 12 million shares were traded. At a price of around $55, this represents a trade value of around $660 million in one day!

OHLC charts

A line chart shows closing prices only and ignores price changes during the frequency period. There can be large price fluctuations during a day's trading, and certainly in a week if you're using a weekly frequency. The OHLC chart allows you to see these price changes because it shows the following key prices:

⇨ O = opening price (first trade price)

⇨ H = highest price

⇨ L = lowest price

⇨ C = closing price (last sale price).

This information is shown on the chart by a vertical line (or bar) where the length of the bar is the range (difference between the highest and lowest prices). Small horizontal bars are shown on each side of the vertical line; the one on the left is the opening price and the one to the right is the closing price. If you're using a daily frequency, each vertical bar is one day's trading and the next day a new bar will be drawn alongside and to the right of the previous bar. If you're using a weekly frequency, there'll be a new bar for each week and then the opening price will be the first sale price at the start of the week, and so on.

The possible variations in OHLC price bars are shown in figure 2.6 (overleaf).

The top bar in figure 2.6 shows the situation where the closing price is higher than the opening price and both the opening and closing prices are within the range between the high and low.

Figure 2.6: OHLC price bars

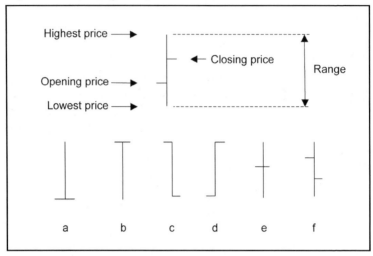

This is by no means the most common scenario; variations that occur, as shown in figure 2.6, are:

⇨ a: after opening, the price rose and then fell to close at the opening price

⇨ b: after opening, the price fell and then rose to close at the opening price

⇨ c: after opening, the price fell to close at the lowest price

⇨ d: after opening, the price rose to close at the highest price

⇨ e: after opening, the price rose and fell and rose again to close at the opening price (or else the price fell, and rose and fell again)

⇨ f: after opening, the price rose and fell and rose again to close below the opening price (or else the price fell and rose and fell again).

With bars 'e' and 'f' you can't tell the sequence of price change. Also, in the top bar of figure 2.6, two scenarios are possible:

⇨ after opening, the price fell to the lowest price then rose to the highest and fell again to close above the opening price

⇨ after opening, the price rose to the highest price then fell to the lowest and rose again to close above the opening price.

In many OHLC charts the bars are coloured—typically blue (or green) and red. These colours are used to distinguish up days and down days (or up weeks and down weeks if you're using weekly frequency). The following conventions are used:

⇨ up day (or up week): closing price is higher than the opening price

⇨ down day (or down week): closing price is lower than the opening price.

Tip

The OHLC chart shows more information than the line chart and is often a better type of chart to use.

Example 4

An example of an OHLC chart is shown in figure 2.7 (overleaf). It's from the CommSec site and is for Tabcorp over a six-month period with a frequency of one day.

If you examine this chart closely you'll see most of the OHLC bar price scenarios that I've mentioned.

Gaps

In figure 2.7 you'll notice an interesting feature that I've marked—a fairly large gap. A gap occurs when the trading range is outside the previous range; that's to say, there's a sudden jump in price either up or down from one day to the next (or one week to the next for a weekly frequency). Gaps aren't shown on a line chart so it's another important advantage of the OHLC chart.

Figure 2.7: OHLC Chart

Source: www.CommSec.com.au

Small gaps occur frequently and aren't usually significant, whereas large gaps indicate a sudden and dramatic change in sentiment and are usually significant — particularly when they're accompanied by high volume. Large gaps generally occur when the market becomes aware of a significant change in announced (or projected) profitability, which reflects in the share price. Other changes causing price gaps include the gain or loss of a major contract or customer, a major change in operations or top management or the announcement (or rumour) of a takeover. With a takeover the gap is usually upward because the predator will need to offer a higher price than the current price if the takeover is likely to succeed. On the other hand, the predator's price may gap down if the market takes the view that the offer price is too high.

ASX rules require that any major change is announced and made available to all investors simultaneously, so when you see a large gap on a chart or a sudden and dramatic rise or fall in price, check company announcements to try to ascertain the reason. Company announcements are accessible on many websites, including the ASX site and online trading sites. However, if the gap or jump is due to rumour or speculation you may not be able to ascertain the cause because there's no announcement.

Tip

Large gaps are usually significant and aren't evident in a line chart. When you see a large gap or rapid change in share price, check company announcements around this time to try to ascertain the cause.

Candle charts

A problem with the OHLC chart is that the horizontal bars are small and can be rather difficult to see and interpret. The candle chart (or candlestick chart) makes interpretation easier because a wide bar is superimposed on the thin bar drawn between the opening and closing prices. The wide bar is known as the body and the thin bar is known as the shadow or wick, so the candle chart is so named because the body and wick can resemble a candle. The body is colour coded—typically an up day (or week) in white, green or blue and a down day (or week) in black or red. Depending on the software you may be able to customise the colours.

Up days and down days are defined in a candle chart in the same way as in an OHLC chart. It's important to realise that this doesn't preclude the possibility that closing prices can fall on an up day or rise on a down day. In fact, this frequently happens. For example, consider the following scenario:

⇨ yesterday's close: $2.54

⇨ today's opening: $2.50

⇨ today's close: $2.52.

On an OHLC or candle chart, today will appear as an up day because today's closing price is higher than today's opening price, but on a line chart the price line will trend down because today's close is lower than yesterday's close.

Example 5

An example of a candle chart is shown in figure 2.8.

Figure 2.8: candle chart

Source: www.CommSec.com.au

This chart from the CommSec site is for Tabcorp for a time period of one year with a frequency of one day.

You can see how difficult it is to distinguish the candles as they all tend to merge together. This is a problem with the candle chart with daily frequency with time periods around one year or more. There are two ways around this problem:

⇨ use a shorter time period

⇨ use a longer frequency.

With OHLC charts over longer time periods the bars also tend to merge so you may need to change the time period or frequency for greater clarity.

Example 6

I've shown you the first option—a shorter time period—in figure 2.9. It's also for Tabcorp but now the time period is only three months.

Figure 2.9: candle chart with shorter time period

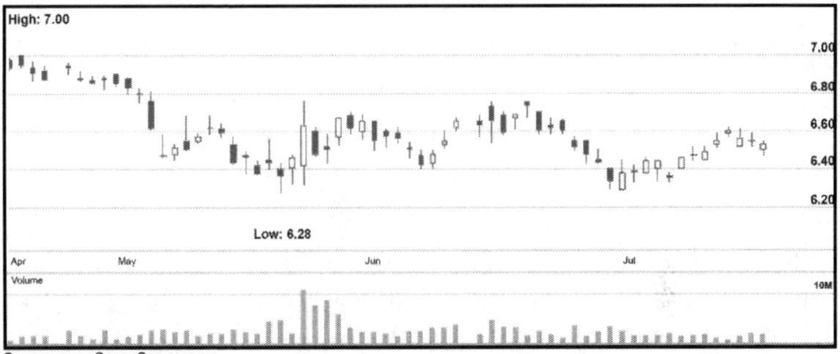

Source: www.CommSec.com.au

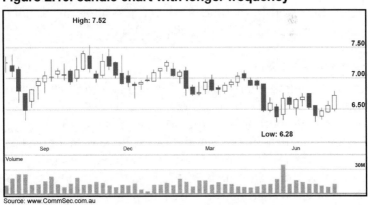

Example 7

The second option is shown in figure 2.10. It's the same time period of one year as in figure 2.8 but now I've changed the frequency to one week.

Figure 2.10: candle chart with longer frequency

Source: www.CommSec.com.au

You can see that in figures 2.9 and 2.10 the bars now stand out clearly and the charts are far easier to interpret.

Tip

The candle chart gives the same information as the OHLC chart and is easier to interpret, but you need to choose the time period and frequency that provide the best clarity.

Candle chart theory

Candle chart theory is a field of study in its own right, with special names given to the various candle shapes and patterns. For example, in figure 2.6 shape 'e' on a candle chart is known as a doji, shape 'a' as a gravestone doji and shape 'b' as a dragonfly doji. When different shapes occur in sequence and form a pattern, names are used such as dark cloud cover, evening star and morning star.

Some chartists are devotees of candle chart theory but in my experience the various shapes and patterns don't give sufficiently reliable indications to provide useful trading signals. However, I use candle charts for fairly short time frame charts because up days and down days stand out most clearly. If you want to explore candle chart theory there are many books on the subject, and the CommSec site has a reasonably extensive outline of the various candle shapes and basic patterns in the 'Charting help' section.

Equi-volume chart

An equi-volume chart is essentially a bar chart where the length of the bar is the price range and where the width of the bar is proportional to the volume of trades. This gives you an immediate impression of trade volume without having to project below the price line to the volume bars to try to match them up. The catch is that because the width of the bars varies, the chart doesn't have a linear time scale.

Example 8

An example of an equi-volume chart is shown in figure 2.11.

Figure 2.11: equi-volume chart

Source: IncredibleCharts.com

This chart is for Westpac Bank (WBC) over a six-month time period, and has been taken from the Incredible Charts site. In this chart, the dates shown on the x axis give you an idea of the date but, as I said, the time scale isn't a linear one.

The bars are coloured with blue indicating up days and red indicating down days. Unfortunately, because all diagrams in this book are black and white you won't easily be able to detect the difference in figure 2.11. Each bar allows you to see opening and closing prices as well as high and low prices, because the bar is coloured only between opening and closing prices.

Equi-volume charts aren't available on the CommSec site.

Equi-volume charts and their interpretation are discussed in greater detail in chapter 9.

Tip

Equi-volume charts provide a good visual representation of the volume accompanying price moves and are well worth a look.

Percent charts

As I've explained, the most useful measure of capital gain (or loss) is the percentage change in price rather than the dollar change. A percent chart allows you to see this at a glance. It's drawn as a line chart with the extreme left starting point of zero percent, and from then on the percentage change in price up or down from the starting price is charted.

Because this chart shows percentage change it enables you to compare capital gains between two different shares on an apples-to-apples basis even when the prices are very different. You can also compare the performance of shares with that of a sector or market index. The number of simultaneous lines you can call up on the one chart depends on the charting software but you're usually able to display at least three lines.

Example 9

An example of a percent chart comparing shares and indices is shown in figure 2.12.

Figure 2.12: percent chart

Source: www.CommSec.com.au

This chart from the CommSec site is for Westpac Bank (WBC) over a six-month period, and I've compared the price change of these shares to the Financials (excluding property trusts) index (XXJ) and the All Ords index (XAO). You can see that in the period from February to May the WBC shares outperformed the indices but then dropped back and closely followed the movement of the indices. The volume bar display is for the volume of WBC shares.

Tip

Use percent charts when you want to look at relative changes or when you want to compare different shares to one another or one or more shares with indices.

Point and figure charts

A point and figure chart is very different to the other charts I've discussed. Price changes are shown only when the price changes by some significant interval—called the box size —that depends upon the price of the shares. For example, if the shares were trading at around $20 a significant price change would be around 50¢, but if the shares were trading at around $1.00 a significant price change would be about 2¢. If the price changes by at least one box size a new point is drawn on the chart, and if the price rises the new point is above the previous one and usually shown in green and/or by a small cross (×). If the price falls the new point is drawn below the previous one and is usually shown in red and/or by a small circle (O). However, these symbols and colours depend on the charting software.

When there's a reversal in the price (from up to down or down to up) a new column is started, but only if the price change is at least equal to another interval known as the reversal. The reversal can be the same as the box size but is usually greater—a default value of three times is common. For example, if the box size is 2¢ a default reversal would be 6¢. The charting software may allow you to change the box size and reversal if you want to.

Example 10

An example of a point and figure chart is shown in figure 2.13.

Figure 2.13: point and figure chart

Source: IncredibleCharts.com

This chart is for Westpac Bank over a six-month period and was taken from the Incredible Charts site (the CommSec site doesn't provide these charts).

The x axis is not time-based; the dates shown are only to allow you to get an approximate date.

On the Incredible Charts site, squares are used (rather than circles) for the down moves. Because the chart in this book isn't coloured it's difficult to detect the up and down days. This isn't a problem when you can see the colours.

Tip

It can be easier to see trends and trend changes on a point and figure chart than with other types of charts. (I'll discuss trends and trend changes in the next chapter.)

What type of chart should I use?

With so many different types of charts available, you're probably wondering which of them you should use. There's no simple answer to this question as each chart type has advantages and limitations. In the first place you're governed by the charting software, and many sites don't provide all the charts I've discussed. So your first step is to explore the site and determine which charts are available and the amount of customisation possible. Then it's really a matter of experimentation to decide which type of chart gives you the information you want in the most easily interpretable way. I'll provide further guidance and suggestions in chapter 12.

Tip

A huge advantage of accessing charts on the internet is that you can experiment with different types of charts and vary the parameters and come to your own conclusions. Before you read later chapters I suggest you spend some time exploring different sites and experimenting with the chart types and parameters.

Chapter summary

⇨ A price chart shows price on the vertical (y) axis and time on the horizontal (x) axis.

⇨ A linear price scale is most common but a logarithmic price scale may be available. This scale shows more clearly the percentage price change rather than the dollar change.

⇨ There are many different types of charts based on price, the most common ones being line charts, OHLC charts, candle charts, equi-volume charts, percent charts and point and figure charts.

⇨ Volume is usually shown as a separate bar chart below the share price.

⇨ Time periods vary widely from a single day (intra-day chart) up to 10 years, or even all data. The time period and frequency you use depends on your purpose. Generally speaking, use a longer time period for longer term investing and shorter time periods for short-term trades. Use the intra-day chart if you're considering placing an order.

⇨ In the line and mountain chart, closing prices are shown and joined with straight lines so the chart appears as a jagged line. There's no indication of how prices changed during a trading period and gaps aren't shown.

⇨ In the OHLC chart, a vertical line shows the range of prices during the trading period with small horizontal bars on each side of the line. The one to the left is the opening price and the one to the right is the closing price.

⇨ The candle chart is a variation of the OHLC chart where the bars between the opening and closing prices are filled in and coloured to indicate whether the closing price is higher or lower than the opening price.

⇨ An advantage of using a chart that shows the range of prices (and not just closing prices) is that gaps can be seen. Small gaps occur frequently and aren't usually of much significance, whereas large gaps are significant and usually indicate a major change that's just been announced or is rumoured.

⇨ A problem with both the OHLC and candle charts is that the vertical bars may be so close together that they almost merge and interpretation becomes difficult. There are two solutions to this problem: use a shorter time period or a longer frequency.

⇨ The equi-volume chart is a variation of the candle chart in which the width of the bars varies according to the volume. This provides an immediate correlation between price change and volume.

⇨ The percent chart is a line chart except that it shows percentage change rather than dollar change so it provides a measure of capital gains as a percentage of capital invested. It also allows you to compare different shares or shares with indices on an apples-to-apples basis, since all lines start at the same point.

⇨ The point and figure chart is a type of bar chart but the x axis is not time based. Instead price moves are shown by symbols and/or colours. The advantage of this chart is that it may allow you to identify trends more easily.

⇨ Each chart type has advantages and disadvantages so you need to experiment and decide which format provides the information you want in the most easily identifiable form, depending on the purpose of your trade. Also vary the time periods and frequencies to see for yourself the effects of doing so.

chapter 3

Trends

In the previous chapter I discussed the different types of charts used in technical analysis. In this chapter, I'll discuss how you can interpret charts to identify trends. I'll also discuss some trend trading strategies you can use.

Trends

The sharemarket is a free market with little regulatory control over buyers and sellers, and consequently the price and volume change with each transaction according to trader sentiment. The day-to-day price and volume changes can look like ripples that have no real significance and appear almost random. They're known as static or white noise because it's rather like the random static or noise you can get with a radio or television receiver. If there's a sustained move in one direction or another, this is a trend and it's an indication of significant market sentiment.

A useful analogy is to imagine you're in a car driving along a smooth road. The trend is the slope of the road which can be level (horizontal) or upward or downward sloping. Now suppose the road is bumpy instead of smooth. The car moves up and down over the bumps but the basic slope isn't affected by them. The ripples in share price and volume are very similar to bumps in a road because they're short-term fluctuations that don't indicate a trend. A trend occurs only when there's a sustained move in some direction.

Tip

It's essential to distinguish trends from the day-to-day ripples or static that are an inevitable part of trading.

Basic trends

There are only three basic trends that can occur:

⇨ horizontal or sideways trend — this is also known as trendless (or directionless)

⇨ uptrend — a move in an upward direction

⇨ downtrend — a move in a downward direction.

A trend is usually drawn as a straight line on a chart, but a trend can also be curved. For simplicity's sake, a curved trend line can be approximated with a number of straight lines. These possibilities for an uptrend are shown in figure 3.1.

Figure 3.1: straight and curved trendlines

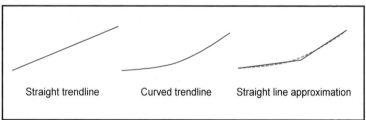

| Straight trendline | Curved trendline | Straight line approximation |

You can see that you can approximate a curved trend very closely with straight lines.

Tip

Charting software may allow you to draw trendlines electronically on a chart and save them for future reference, but in most cases you'll be able to draw straight lines only.

Identifying trends: best fit method

One method of drawing a trendline is as a line of best fit. There are mathematical procedures for calculating a line of best fit (regression analysis) and some charting software includes it. Such precision isn't usually necessary, and you can draw a line of best fit by 'eye'; that is, by visual interpretation. If the charting software gives you the option of drawing the line on the screen, you place the cursor at a start point and then draw the line to an end point. If you're not happy with the line you can delete it and try again. If you can't draw the line on your computer screen you can print a hard copy of the chart and use a ruler and pencil.

In figure 3.2 I've drawn a straight line of best fit using visual interpretation through a number of data points.

Figure 3.2: line of best fit using visual interpretation

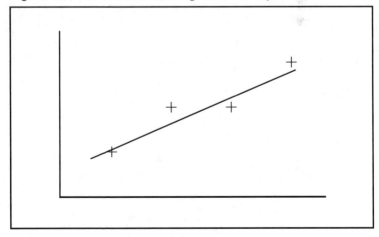

Tip

If you're drawing trendlines on a paper chart, it's best to use a transparent ruler.

Outside points

Sometimes you'll find points that don't seem to fit into a trend. In figure 3.3 I've identified an outside point 'x' that doesn't seem to fit into the uptrend as indicated by the other points.

Figure 3.3: outside point

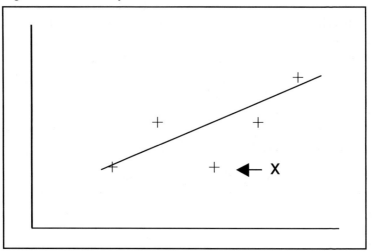

When this occurs you have two options:

⇨ ignore the outside point and regard it as an aberration (as I've done in figure 3.3)

⇨ include the data point and adjust the line of best fit accordingly. If you choose this option, the other points won't fit as well into the trendline.

There's no clear-cut way of deciding which of these options is most accurate so you'll need to use your own discretion.

Tip

When outside points occur on a chart when you're identifying a trendline, try excluding the points and then
including them and compare the lines to see which seems
to best fit the data.

Volume trends

You can also identify a volume trend using the best fit method
by joining the ends of the volume bars in a volume chart. In
figure 3.4 I've shown two volume trendlines.

Figure 3.4: volume trends

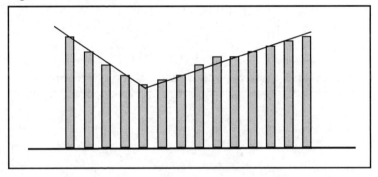

Volume trends aren't usually as sustained as price trends and
the volume bars may seem to change in an almost random
fashion without any clear trend being apparent. There can be
volume spikes that accompany significant price changes but
at times there seems no logical correlation between them. I'll
discuss these effects in greater detail in chapter 9.

Example 1

Let's now look at a share price chart with a trendline of best fit,
shown in figure 3.5 (overleaf). The chart is a line (mountain)
chart from the CommSec site for Adelaide Brighton (ABC)
over a six-month period.

Figure 3.5: line (mountain) chart with trendline

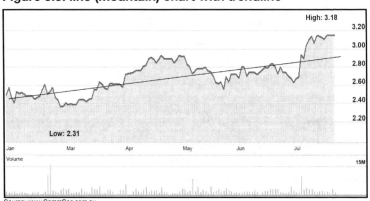

Source: www.CommSec.com.au

I've drawn a single trendline on the chart but I could also have drawn a number of them. I've shown this option in figure 3.6.

Figure 3.6: line (mountain) chart with multiple trendlines

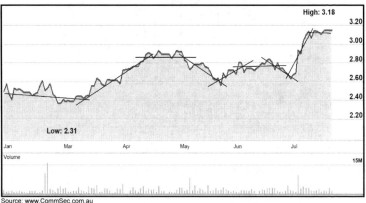

Source: www.CommSec.com.au

Which method should I use?

Whether you want to draw a single trendline or multiple ones is largely a question of the time period of the investment or trade. For longer term investing you're most interested in the overall trend so a single trendline may do, but usually you'll need to use more than one line to accurately reflect trends.

Identifying trends: high–low method

Another way of identifying trends is to use an OHLC or candle chart and join the upper or lower ends of the price range bars. Use the following criteria to identify uptrends and downtrends:

⇨ in an uptrend the lows are higher

⇨ in a downtrend the highs are lower.

These criteria can't be applied in a sidetrend when both the lows and the highs are at approximately the same level. Then I suggest you use low points at the same level as the criteria for identifying a sidetrend.

When using the high–low criteria for identifying a trend you won't be able to use all bars, but at least three of them should touch the line. Some bars may overlap the line a little so you need to use judgement when drawing the trendline.

Identifying a trend using the high–low method is illustrated in figure 3.7.

Figure 3.7: trend identification using the high–low method

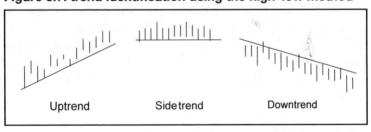

Uptrend   Side trend   Downtrend

You might be wondering why you should identify uptrends by joining the lows and downtrends by joining the highs, and not the other way round. There's a logical reason for this: a significant break in an uptrend occurs when new lows aren't higher than previous lows—that's to say the price lows break the trendline downward. Similarly, a break in a downtrend occurs when new highs aren't lower than previous highs—the price highs break upward away from the trendline.

I've illustrated these principles in figure 3.8.

Figure 3.8: uptrend and downtrend breakouts

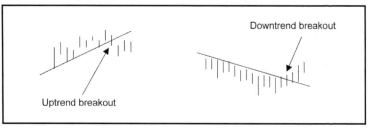

Tip

When using the high–low method for trend identification, join the price lows to identify an uptrend and join the price highs to identify a downtrend. Breaks of trend occur when price bars break through the trendline—down through an uptrend line and up through a downtrend line.

Channels

In an uptrend the price highs as well as the lows usually trend upward, and in a downtrend the price lows as well as the highs usually trend downward. When this occurs you'll be able to join both the high and low ends of the price bars to form a channel with parallel (or approximately parallel) sides. I've shown this in figure 3.9.

Figure 3.9: channels

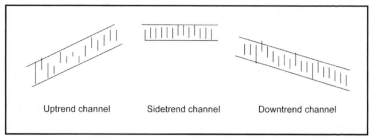

Tip

In an uptrend channel use the lower line for defining the trendline and in a downtrend channel use the upper line.

Support and resistance levels

In a sidetrend channel the lower and upper lines have special significance. The lower line is known as a support level and the upper line as a resistance level. These are shown in figure 3.10.

Figure 3.10: support and resistance levels

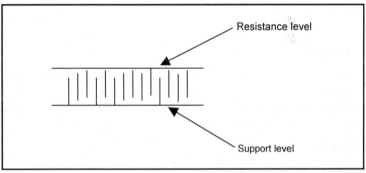

As you might infer from the names, if the price falls to the support level traders will buy the shares because they're regarded as good value at this price. Buying pressure supports the price so it doesn't fall any lower. On the other hand, the resistance level is the price at which there's buyer resistance so the price won't rise any higher. In a prolonged sidetrend this state of affairs continues for a considerable period, with the share price bouncing around between support and resistance levels like a ball bouncing between floors in a multi-storey car park.

Tip

Sidetrends often occur as channels with parallel support and resistance lines.

Support and resistance in uptrends and downtrends

The concept of support and resistance levels in a sidetrend can be modified and applied to uptrends and downtrends, as follows:

⇨ uptrend: the support line is inclined upward

⇨ downtrend: the resistance line is inclined downward.

Tip

You can view an uptrend as a trend where the support line is angled upward and a downtrend as a trend where the resistance line is angled downward.

Example 2

Let's now look at a share price chart with trendlines using the high–low method, in figure 3.11. For comparison purposes I've used the same chart of Adelaide Brighton as previously except that the chart is now in OHLC format rather than in line chart format.

Figure 3.11: OHLC chart with trendlines

Source: www.CommSec.com.au

You can see that you can't logically draw a single uptrend or downtrend line through all the bars; it's necessary to draw multiple trendlines. There's a gap I've marked, and when a gap occurs it's usually necessary to identify another trendline.

There's also a horizontal space in April but it's not a price gap —it's a trading break due to the Easter holiday.

Let's now look at this chart again and see if trend channels can be identified (see figure 3.12).

Figure 3.12: OHLC chart with trend channels

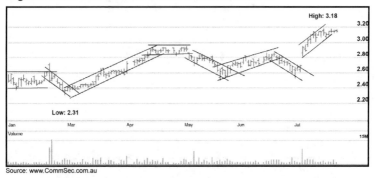

Source: www.CommSec.com.au

You can see that channels can be drawn with approximately parallel support and resistance lines. This isn't always the case but it's a very common scenario.

Tip

You can often join both the tops and bottoms of price bars to form channels with parallel sides. Breakouts from a prolonged channel formation are generally significant and indicate a major change in sentiment.

Wedges

It's not always the case that support and resistance lines are parallel and form channels. If they're not parallel, this is known as a wedge, triangle or pennant, and they can be converging or diverging, as shown in figure 3.13 (overleaf).

There are many possible variations, depending on the inclination of the support and resistance lines. I've illustrated only six: 'a', 'b' and 'c' are converging wedges and 'd', 'e' and 'f' are diverging ones.

Figure 3.13: wedges

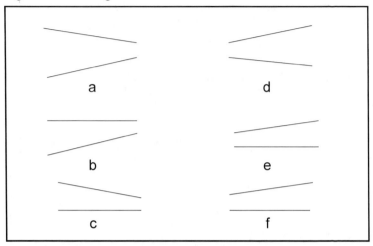

Converging and diverging wedges can be interpreted as follows:

⇨ converging wedge: decreasing price volatility indicating a move toward consensus of a fair price

⇨ diverging wedge: increasing price volatility indicating a move away from consensus of a fair price.

Tip

Converging and diverging wedges aren't usually sustained for long before there's a break out above or below the support or resistance line. These breakouts (particularly from a converging wedge) often herald a major change in sentiment and can be regarded as significant trading signals.

Trend identification in a point and figure chart

As I mentioned in chapter 2, an advantage of the point and figure chart is that it's often easier to identify trends and trend changes. When using a point and figure chart, identify trends using the high–low method by joining the bottoms of the columns for an uptrend, the tops of the columns for a downtrend and both tops and bottoms for channels or wedges.

Example 3

Let's now look at a point and figure chart with trendlines, in figure 3.14. This is the chart for Westpac (WBC) from chapter 2, taken from the Incredible Charts site. It covers a period of 18 months and the box size is one and the reversal is three.

Figure 3.14: point and figure chart with trendlines

Source: IncredibleCharts.com

There are several converging wedges, and you can see that the price breakout from each one indicated a significant trend change.

Tip

Practise your trend identification skills by obtaining charts in several different formats and drawing trendlines and trend channels. If the charting software doesn't allow you to draw the lines on the screen, you'll need to print a hard copy and use the pencil and ruler method.

Trend trading strategies

It's all very interesting to obtain charts and identify trends and channels but there's no point to it unless you can use your identification skills with trading strategies. I'll now propose some trading strategies based on trend identification.

The basic trend trading strategy derives from the well-known market saying 'the trend is your friend'. That's to say, go with the flow rather than against it. A trend is similar to a tidal flow in a river and you'll make more headway by swimming with the flow rather than by swimming against it. Going against the flow is known as a contrarian strategy and it can be a way of obtaining superior returns (beating the market) in some instances; for example, when a trend unexpectedly changes direction. But in the long run it's generally safer to trade with the trend than to go against it.

You can adopt the following strategy:

> Buy (go long) in an uptrend. Don't buy in a down-trend, sell if you are currently holding or go short.

This strategy is virtually infallible in a sustained uptrend, provided that you buy early enough in the uptrend and sell quickly enough should the trend falter. To do this you need to detect the uptrend in its early stages and ride the trend long enough to make a worthwhile profit. Also you need to quickly identify when the uptrend falters and sell before your gains are eroded too much. Stop loss orders may be used for this purpose as they result in an automatic sale should the price fall below the level you set.

Tip

If you're not familiar with stop loss orders or you haven't used them, you really need to get up to speed. My books Online Investing on the Australian Sharemarket *and* Teach Yourself About Shares *provide information about these orders as well as other types of conditional orders.*

Multi-parcel buying

If you're not confident about an uptrend you can buy multiple parcels at different points in time—a strategy known as cost averaging. If you adjust the buy quantity as the price changes so that the parcel value remains the same it's known as dollar cost averaging.

Multi-parcel buying reduces the downside risk should an uptrend falter soon after you've bought in, but it will reduce profit if you were correct in your initial analysis and the trend continues upward after your initial purchase.

Tip

If you've bought and the price falls, don't attempt to cost average by holding on to the shares you've bought and buying some more shares at the lower price unless you're confident that the downtrend has reversed.

Selling in an uptrend

Some traders advocate setting profit targets and selling in an uptrend when the price reaches the target. For example, you might buy some shares for $10.00 and set a profit target of 25%, so that if the price rises to $12.50 you'll sell and take profits. Traders who use this strategy may use another type of conditional order known as a profit stop, which is an automatic sell transaction. (My other books also deal with these orders.)

The purpose of this strategy is to cash in profits and avoid losses should an uptrend reverse. While this seems a reasonable approach, I don't support it because I want to make as much profit as possible in an uptrend. Not all trades are profitable, and it's necessary to have some high-profit trades to more than compensate for losing ones. If you can make more profit by riding a trend, why not do so for as long as you can?

Tip

After buying into an uptrend, ride the trend for as long as you can and don't cash in profits until the trend falters.

Multi-parcel selling

A multi-parcel strategy can also be used with selling. You use this strategy by selling in multiple parcels rather than all shares at once. This strategy reduces the risk of lost profits if the downtrend isn't sustained and the price rises after you've sold the first parcel. But if the downtrend is sustained, multi-parcel selling reduces your profit.

Tip

Use a multi-parcel selling strategy only if you're not confident that a downtrend will be sustained.

Sidetrend channel trading

When prices are trending sideways, it doesn't mean that you shouldn't trade because trend trading profits can't be made. As long as a sidetrend channel persists and prices bounce between support and resistance levels you can make short-term profits by buying when the price is around the support level and selling when the price is around the resistance level.

The sidetrend channel trading strategy is illustrated in figure 3.15.

Figure 3.15: buying and selling in a sidetrend channel

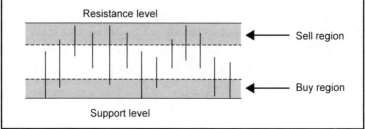

The percentage profit may be low but the time period may also be short, so the annualised profit can still be very good (refer back to the short-term profit example in chapter 1).

Uptrend channel trading

The same basic strategy can be used in an uptrending channel. As well as profiting from the uptrend you can increase your profit by buying near the low of the channel and selling near the top. On the other hand, if you buy near the top of the channel and sell near the bottom, you mightn't even make a profit on the trade if the channel slope isn't very steep. This is illustrated in figure 3.16.

Figure 3.16: loss trade in an uptrend channel

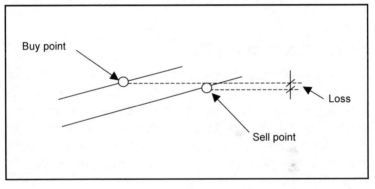

Even though you adopt the basically sound strategy of buying in an uptrend, you can still make a loss if you buy near the resistance level and sell later near the support level.

Tip

Most profit is made in an uptrending channel when you buy near the support level and sell near the resistance level.

Wedge breakout trading

There's no really reliable trading strategy when the price is in a diverging or converging wedge formation. The wedge formation isn't usually of prolonged duration, so if there are no other considerations it's best to wait for a breakout before trading. A break out from a converging wedge is usually significant. If the price breaks upward that's often a good buy signal, and a downward breakout is often a good sell signal. A break out from a diverging wedge isn't usually significant and is not a reliable trading signal.

Tip

Avoid trading in wedges (especially divergent ones); wait until a wedge breakout occurs.

Interpretation of trends

Sometimes when you look at a chart a trend will be obvious and you can identify it with confidence. At other times you won't be so sure and then it's possible to draw different conclusions. So it's important to realise that there's no single correct interpretation of a chart in technical analysis. There's an element of subjectivity in the identification of trends, and different analysts could examine the same chart and draw different trendlines. It's a problem I'll discuss in greater detail in later chapters and I'll also include some examples.

Chapter summary

⇨ A trend is a sustained move in one direction. The three basic trends are uptrends, downtrends and sidetrends.

⇨ Trendlines can be curved, but most often are drawn as straight lines. A series of straight trendlines can give a good approximation of a curved trendline.

⇨ One way of drawing a trendline is a line of best fit. If one or more points seem abnormal, you need to decide whether to include or exclude them.

⇨ Volume trends can be identified by joining the ends of the bars on a volume chart. However, volume trends are usually of short duration and not as sustained as price trends, and can appear to be almost random.

⇨ The number of trendlines you draw on a chart is a matter of personal preference.

⇨ Longer term investors are more interested in longer term trends whereas shorter term traders will want to identify the shorter trends.

⇨ A common way of identifying trends is the high–low method. This can be done only with a chart showing the range of prices during each trading period. Uptrends are identified by joining price bar lows and the trendline slopes upward. Downtrends are identified by joining price bar highs and the trendline slopes downward.

⇨ If you join the tops and bottoms of price bars and the lines are approximately parallel, this is known as a channel and it's a very common feature in most charts.

⇨ In a channel, the lower line is regarded as a support level and the upper line as a resistance level. Prices often bounce around between support and resistance for a sustained period.

⇨ If the sides of a channel aren't parallel this is known as a wedge, triangle or pennant, and can be converging or diverging.

⇨ Trends are often identified more easily using a point and figure chart.

⇨ The most reliable trend trading strategy is to trade with the trend. Contrarians trade against the trend; sometimes this can produce good results if the trend changes unexpectedly.

⇨ Stop loss orders are a good way of minimising the damage should an uptrend suddenly reverse.

⇨ Riding an uptrend for as long as possible maximises profitability, but some traders cash in profits and sell while the uptrend is still in progress. They may use profit stop orders for this purpose.

⇨ Multi-parcel buying or selling reduces risk but it can also reduce profits if the trend is sustained.

⇨ In a sidetrend channel you can make short-term trading profits by buying near the support level and selling near the resistance level.

⇨ You make most profit in an uptrending channel if you buy near the support level and sell near the resistance level.

⇨ Wedge formations don't usually last for very long, and it's best to wait until the formation breaks before trading.

chapter 4

Patterns

In chapter 3 I discussed basic chart trends and trading strategies based on them. In this chapter I'll discuss trend changes and common chart patterns that occur with trend changes. I'll also outline some trading strategies you can use when you identify patterns.

Chart patterns

A pattern is a recognisable shape that appears in a chart; that is, a sequence that recurs periodically in one chart or from one chart to another. Because patterns are recurring changes, if you can recognise them you're able to forecast the most likely future scenario and improve the likelihood of successful trades.

It's rather like a synoptic chart used with weather forecasting. To the untrained eye it's just a series of lines joining points of equal pressure. However, a meteorologist can recognise patterns in the chart and draw on past experience with similar patterns to forecast the likely impact on the weather.

Trading strategies based on patterns involve four steps. These are:

⇨ examine the chart to identify trend changes and patterns

⇨ use your pattern recognition skills to forecast the most likely future scenario

⇨ develop trading strategies based on your forecast

⇨ implement your strategies; that is, place your buy or sell orders.

Trend changes

Patterns are based on one or more trend changes. Before I look at the various patterns that can occur, the question that needs to be answered is: can a trend continue indefinitely or will it always change? This question doesn't have a simple answer, so I'll consider it in relation to the three basic trends examined in chapter 3: uptrends, sidetrends and downtrends.

Uptrend change

In principle, there's no reason why an uptrend can't continue indefinitely. A sustainable uptrend is one that's reasonable and justified. To decide whether or not an uptrend is justified you need to consider the basic principle underlying share prices: the true value of a business is the present worth of all its future earnings (profits), and the true worth of a share in the business is the present worth of all future earnings divided by the number of shares on issue; that's to say, the present worth of all future earnings per share (EPS).

The concept of present worth comes about because future profits aren't as valuable as present profits, so future profits need to be discounted to evaluate them fairly now.

If a business enterprise can continue to grow profits the share price should continue to rise, and this will appear as a long-term price uptrend in a chart. This occurs because share price is closely related to the earnings per share by a statistic known as the price to earnings ratio (PE) that tends to remain reasonably constant. So if EPS keeps growing the share price should keep rising. On the other hand, if future profits are based on blue sky potential and the business fails to deliver, sooner or later a price uptrend will falter. This type of correction will also occur if the market or a share becomes overheated and rises too far away from a justifiable value.

These effects can be seen very clearly in a long-term chart of the All Ordinaries index, as shown in figure 4.1.

Figure 4.1: All Ords long-term trend

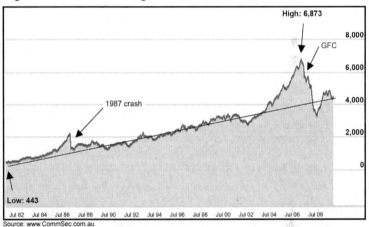

Source: www.CommSec.com.au

In this chart (from the CommSec site) I've added a trendline and you can see that there's been a long-term uptrend. This indicates that over this period major Australian companies were able to grow their profits in a sustainable fashion. However, there were two significant corrections to the uptrend. The first was the 1987 crash, and the second was due to the global financial crisis (GFC).

There are two interesting features about these corrections:

⇨ In both cases, the correction was preceded by a steep rise above the long-term trendline; that is, overheating. So you could say that the correction in both cases was inevitable even though they both had very different causes.

⇨ The GFC crash is a good example of over-correction. You can see that the price dropped below the long-term trendline for a period before correcting back to it.

I've illustrated these effects in figure 4.2.

Figure 4.2: overheating correction

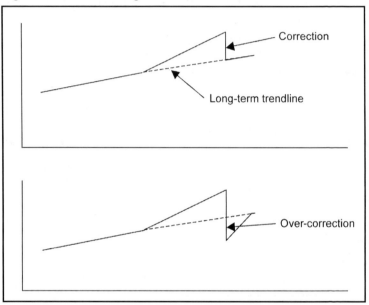

Tip

When unjustifiable uptrends occur, there's bound to be a correction. Unjustifiable uptrends are often indicated on a chart when the price trends steeply up from the long-term trendline.

Effect of a dividend on a trend

For companies that pay a dividend there's always a small correction (drop in share price) when the shares go ex-dividend because the shares become less valuable. Generally speaking, the price will drop by the amount of the dividend, or sometimes by a greater amount due to the benefit of franking credits (if the dividend is franked). For example, if today's closing price is $2.34 and the dividend per share is 7¢, if the shares trade ex-dividend tomorrow you can expect the opening price to be about $2.27.

The difference between a correction due to a dividend and one due to overheating is that the dividend correction is much smaller and occurs at regular intervals: every six months, corresponding to the interim and final ex-dividend dates.

Tip

If you notice a sudden drop in price for the shares in a company that pays a dividend, check whether this drop is due to the dividend. Some charting software (such as CommSec) allows you to highlight dividends on a price chart.

Sidetrend change

A share price that's in a sidetrend channel is also known as trendless, for the obvious reason that the share price isn't going anywhere and is just bouncing around between support and resistance levels. The share price is lethargic, with traders and investors perceiving no likelihood of a change in earnings so there's no good reason to push the price either up beyond the resistance level or down below the support level. A break out from the channel is likely only if a significant change occurs (or is likely to occur). If the change is seen as favourable the breakout will be upward or if unfavourable it will be downward, otherwise the sidetrend can continue indefinitely.

Tip

A sidetrend can continue for a long time if no significant change of fortunes occurs.

Downtrend change

There's a major difference between a downtrend and an uptrend or sidetrend: a downtrend can't continue indefinitely.
Sooner or later the price will hit the zero line (or very close
to it) and there's no possibility of the price falling any more.
As that point approaches the company will most likely be
declared bankrupt. This situation is illustrated in figure 4.3.

Figure 4.3: downtrend reaching zero

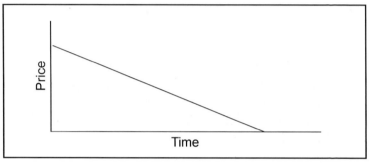

A rather more common scenario is that the fall will flatten out
as the x axis is approached, as shown in figure 4.4.

Figure 4.4: downtrend approaching zero

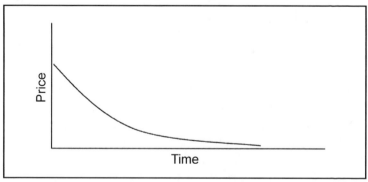

If you were holding the shares you should have sold before
the bottom, but many traders and investors get caught when

they continue holding the shares in the hope that they'll recover. You can also get trapped if you adopt the mindset 'the price has gone as low as it possibly can'. There's never any lowest possible price, other than the shares becoming worthless.

Tip

It's extremely dangerous to assume a share price can't fall any lower than what you think is the lowest possible level. It can, and often will.

Trend change patterns

Now that I've explored the possibility of a trend continuing indefinitely, I'll now look at some of the patterns that can occur when trend changes occur. The first I'll look at is uptrend change patterns.

Uptrend change patterns

I've already described the situation where an uptrend becomes overheated and corrects dramatically downward. This occurs frequently but is by no means the most frequent uptrend change pattern. Two more common ones are:

⇨ uptrend to sidetrend

⇨ uptrend to downtrend.

These are illustrated in figure 4.5.

Figure 4.5: uptrend change patterns

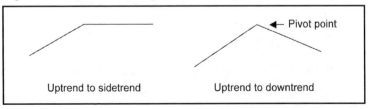

Uptrend to sidetrend   ◄— Pivot point   Uptrend to downtrend

As marked in this diagram, when an uptrend reverses to a downtrend the point at the apex of the change (highest price) is known as the pivot point.

I've illustrated these trend changes using straight lines, but the pattern may be curved with a more gradual transition from one to the other, as shown in figure 4.6.

Figure 4.6: gradual uptrend change patterns

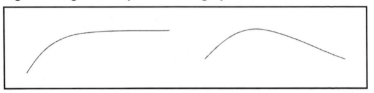

Sidetrend change patterns

As I've said, when a share price is locked in a sideways channel the price can bounce between the support and resistance levels for a considerable time, like a ball bouncing between a roof and a floor. Eventually something will give and the share price will break through—either upward or downward—just as if the ball had found a hole in the roof or the floor. When the price breaks through and is sustained for more than one or two trading sessions the move is generally significant and heralds a major change in trader sentiment.

Tip

A sustained break through an established support or resistance level in a sidetrend is usually significant and indicative of a major change in sentiment.

When the price does break through the support or resistance level, the possible scenarios are:

⇨ sidetrend to sidetrend rise

⇨ sidetrend to sidetrend fall

⇨ sidetrend to uptrend

⇨ sidetrend to downtrend.

These patterns are shown in figure 4.7.

Figure 4.7: sidetrend change patterns

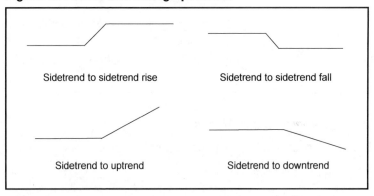

As is the case with the uptrend change pattern, the transition may be smooth rather than sudden as I've shown in this diagram.

New channel support and resistance levels

There's a special case of the sidetrend to sidetrend pattern (either rise or fall) that frequently occurs. The new channel is established with new support or resistance levels, as follows:

⇨ In an upward breakout, the old resistance level becomes the new support level.

⇨ In a downward breakout, the old support level becomes the new resistance level.

These scenarios are illustrated in figure 4.8 (overleaf).

Tip

In a sidetrend to sidetrend channel upward breakout it's frequently the case that the new support level is the old resistance level, and in a downward breakout the new resistance level is the old support level.

Figure 4.8: sidetrend new support and resistance

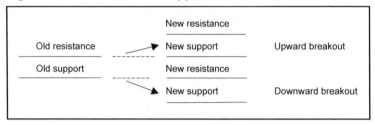

Downtrend change patterns

In a downtrend change, the basic patterns are:

⇨ downtrend to sidetrend

⇨ downtrend to uptrend.

These changes are illustrated in figure 4.9. Like the uptrend change, the transition can be sudden or curved.

Figure 4.9: downtrend change patterns

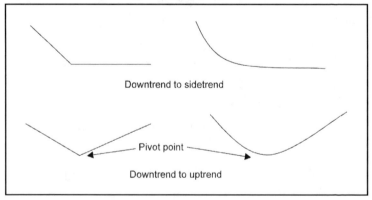

There's a special case of downtrend to sidetrend with speculative shares when the price falls to only a few cents. While the shares are still listed and are being traded, the price may hover around the very low value for a long time before the company either goes bankrupt or experiences a favourable change in fortunes.

Tip

Very cheap shares (penny dreadfuls) offer the possibility of huge profits (on a return on capital basis) if there's a change in fortunes, but they're the most risky of all shares to trade.

Wedge or triangle breakout

As I indicated in chapter 3, a wedge or triangle pattern isn't usually sustained for long. The break out from a diverging wedge isn't usually significant because a diverging wedge indicates increasing price volatility and price uncertainty. By its very nature, a converging wedge can't be sustained because eventually the support and resistance levels would meet. In the convergence there's decreasing volatility, so when the breakout occurs it's usually indicative of a major change in sentiment. The breakout could be upward indicating a positive sentiment change or downward indicating a negative sentiment change. These scenarios are illustrated in figure 4.10.

Figure 4.10: converging wedge or triangle breakouts

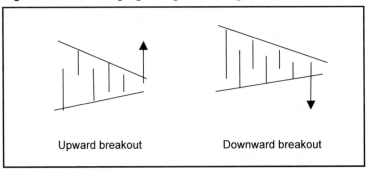

Upward breakout   Downward breakout

After the breakout, the most likely scenarios are:

⇨ uptrend breakout: a new uptrend or sidetrend with higher support and resistance levels will form

⇨ downtrend breakout: a new downtrend or sidetrend with lower support and resistance levels will form.

Tip

A price breakout from a converging wedge or triangle usually indicates a significant change in sentiment, upward if optimistic and downward if pessimistic.

Compound patterns

By now you've probably realised that compound patterns with almost unlimited variations can occur, especially in longer term charts. I've illustrated just a few frequently recurring compound patterns in figure 4.11. I've shown these using straight lines, but as we know the trend change is often curved (transitional) rather than being sudden.

Figure 4.11: compound patterns

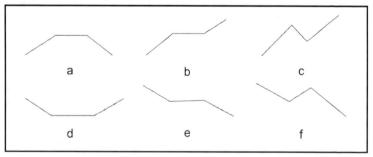

These patterns are:

⇨ a: uptrend–sidetrend–downtrend

⇨ b: uptrend–sidetrend–uptrend

⇨ c: uptrend–downtrend–uptrend

⇨ d: downtrend–sidetrend–uptrend

⇨ e: downtrend–sidetrend–downtrend

⇨ f: downtrend–uptrend–downtrend.

Of these compound patterns, the most vexing ones are 'c' and 'f'. These patterns are known as double reversals because the trend reverses twice. If you trade using the signal given by the first reversal you'll end up in a whipsaw situation because when the trend reverses again you need to trade once more to get back into the uptrend or get out of trouble in the downtrend. This type of double trade involves extra cost and usually results in lower profit compared to a trader not acting on the first trend reversal signal.

Tip

Whipsaw trades result from double reversals and are usually unproductive.

Double tops and bottoms

A special variant of the uptrend to downtrend change is a compound pattern known as the double top that often appears after a prolonged uptrend. The price rises to a resistance level then falls away, before rising back to it and falling again. This time the price doesn't recover and continues to fall. The resistance level is approximately level but can also be inclined a little either up or down. This pattern is shown in figure 4.12.

Figure 4.12: double top pattern

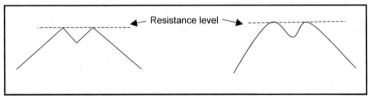

The double top is regarded as a powerful uptrend reversal signal. If you act too quickly when the downtrend appears to reverse the first time, you can end up being whipsawed when the second reversal occurs and the second apparent uptrend turns out to be illusory. After the second reversal you can be fairly confident that a downtrend has now been established and that it's likely to continue for some time.

The double bottom is the inverse of the double top and a powerful downtrend reversal signal. After the second reversal you can be fairly confident that an uptrend has now been established and is likely to continue for some time.

Tip

Double tops or bottoms are usually powerful trend reversal signals.

Triple tops and bottoms

The triple top or bottom is a variant of the double top or bottom pattern that occurs less frequently but is a powerful trend reversal signal after the pattern has been completed. This time the price bounces three times from a support or resistance level. I've illustrated a triple bottom in figure 4.13.

Figure 4.13: triple bottom pattern

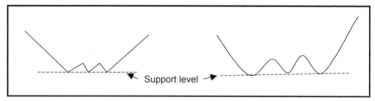

Head and shoulders pattern

The final reversal pattern I'm going to mention is a variant of the triple top or bottom pattern known as the head and shoulders pattern. As the name suggests, this pattern resembles a head with a shoulder on each side above a neckline, as illustrated in figure 4.14.

Figure 4.14: head and shoulders pattern

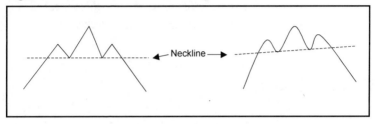

The pattern as illustrated is an uptrend reversal pattern but it can also be inverted and then it becomes a downtrend reversal pattern known as an inverted head and shoulder pattern. It's not a pattern that occurs frequently, but when it does occur it's regarded as a powerful trend reversal signal.

Tip

Triple tops and bottoms, head and shoulders or inverted head and shoulder patterns don't occur very often, but when they do appear they're usually powerful trend reversal signals.

Other patterns

The patterns I've described aren't the only ones possible, and some chartists describe and place significance on other patterns such as diamonds, steeple tops, saucers and mares tails. Devotees of candlestick charting describe other patterns such as dark cloud cover and morning and evening stars.

My advice is that you steer clear of these complications at this stage and stick to the basic trends and patterns I've described. They will serve you well in your analysis and interpretation of charts and you can derive sound trading strategies based on them.

Tip

The basic trend changes and patterns I've described provide a good foundation for technical analysis and trading strategies based on them. More complex pattern recognition won't necessarily improve your analysis.

Fibonacci ratios

Some chartists believe that there's a mathematical sequence to trend reversals deriving from a series known as the Fibonacci series, derived by 13th-century mathematician Leonardo Fibonacci. Fibonacci developed the series to predict the population growth of rabbits in a field. He concluded that the population would grow in the sequence 1, 2, 3, 5, 8, 13, 21, 34, 55 and so on, where each number in the series is the sum of the two previous numbers. For example: $3 = 1 + 2$, $5 = 2 + 3$, $8 = 3 + 5$. Interestingly, although the series involves addition of numbers, after the first few numbers the ratio of successive numbers is approximately the same. These ratios are 1.618 or the inverse 0.618. For example, $21 \div 13 = 1.615$ and $34 \div 21 = 1.619$. Additional significant ratios can be obtained by inverting the significant ratio or by subtraction from 1. For example: $1 \div 1.618 = 0.618$ and $1 - 0.618 = 0.382$.

Some significant Fibonacci ratios (rounded off) are 0.38, 0.62, 1.38 and 1.62, and these ratios can be used to calculate trend turning points. For example, let's say that a share price moves up from a support level of $1.64 to a new support level of $1.98.

Initial upward move: $1.98 − $1.64 = $0.34 = 34¢

Applying the Fibonacci ratios:

⇨ $34 \times 0.38 = 13$

⇨ $34 \times 0.62 = 21$

⇨ $34 \times 1.38 = 47$

⇨ $34 \times 1.62 = 55$

If the price continues to move up, the predicted target price (new resistance level) is: $1.98 + 13¢ = $2.11. If the price continues to move up after reaching this level the next target price is: $1.98 + 21¢ = $2.19. And so on, with the next two target prices of $2.45 and $2.53.

On the other hand, if the price falls a target support price is: $1.98 – 13¢ = $1.85. If the shares don't find support at this level but continue to fall, the next support level is: $1.98 – 21¢ = $1.77.

If the price continues to fall, the next predicted support levels are $1.98 – 47¢ = $1.51 and $1.98 – 55¢ = $1.43.

Predicting support and resistance levels in this way would be a wonderful aid to technical analysis if it was reliable, but I'm extremely dubious about the concept. I believe that any theory or mathematical solution that's been developed for a certain situation can't logically be applied to a totally different situation unless there's some proven correlation between the two. And I can see no logical connection between population growth of rabbits in a field and share prices.

Some claim that Fibonacci ratios work because people believe they work; in other words, that they're a self-fulfilling prophecy. In my example, a trader calculating a target price of $2.11 might place a profit stop order at this level. If many traders adopt the same strategy the selling pressure will cause the price to fall after reaching $2.11, and would appear to support the use of Fibonacci ratios in trading markets.

Self-fulfilling prophecies can occur with share prices, but I've seen no evidence that Fibonacci ratios give more reliable predictions than would occur by random chance. It seems to me that you could use any set of ratios—such as 0.25, 0.5, 0.75, 1.25 and 1.5—and show that on some occasions support and resistance levels occur as predicted by these ratios. But this would be purely coincidental and wouldn't prove that these ratios actually work.

Tip

It's easy enough to test Fibonacci ratios and draw your own conclusions by examining charts and identifying support and resistance levels using the ratios.

Wave patterns

A wave theory was developed by Ralph Elliott in the 1930s proposing that prices move in waves resulting from alternating investor optimism and pessimism in accordance with Fibonacci ratios. A basic uptrend consists of a five-wave advance and a three-wave decline, whereas a downtrend consists of a five-wave decline and a three-wave advance. The waves moving with the trend are called motive waves, whereas the waves moving against it are called corrective waves. An uptrend wave pattern is shown in figure 4.15.

Figure 4.15: basic uptrend wave pattern

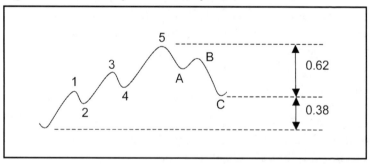

In this diagram, the motive waves are numbered 1 to 5 and the corrective waves are labelled A to C. Each of the waves can be subdivided further into sub-waves, each of which can be subdivided again, so the completed uptrend pattern consists of 89 motive waves followed by 55 corrective waves.

While Elliott theory has many advocates, there's no clear evidence that it's a useful technical analysis tool. Apart from my reservations about applying Fibonacci ratios to shares, another problem with Elliott's theory is that there's no clear-cut way of deciding when a wave sequence starts and ends.

The full Elliott wave theory is too complex to be of value to us but I believe that the underlying principle is a sound one. Trends usually occur in waves (or bounces) rather than steady and smooth lines. I'm not so sure that these waves necessarily result from alternating optimism and pessimism; rather they may simply be caused by day-to-day trading and profit taking. An uptrend can be in place for a number of days before it retraces and loses some of the gains as traders cash in profits, then after the selling pressure subsides the uptrend re-establishes. The same type of situation can occur in downtrends, with wave action rather than a constant price fall each day.

Tip

Trends often occur in waves or bounces rather than as steady rises or falls, and you need to watch for apparent trend changes that are transitory and not significant trend turning points.

Trading strategies using patterns

I've already outlined the basic trend trading strategy, but it's so important that I'll restate it: buy in an uptrend and don't buy in a downtrend. I've also pointed out that some traders believe it's a good strategy to set profit targets and sell when the target is reached, but it's not a strategy I endorse.

Buying strategy

Clearly the best time to buy is when an uptrend starts, and the earlier you can get into the uptrend and the longer the uptrend lasts the more profit you'll make. Most uptrends initiate from a trend change, either a sidetrend–uptrend or downtrend–uptrend change. So you need to identify the initial trend reversal point as soon as possible and ride the trend for as long as you can. However, if you jump in and trade too quickly on an apparent downtrend–uptrend reversal you could end up being whipsawed if the apparent trend reversal is illusory, as shown in figure 4.16.

Figure 4.16: whipsaw trade on apparent downtrend–uptrend reversal

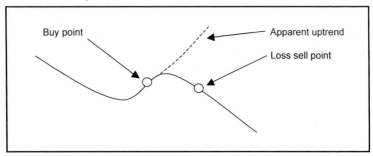

A false bounce from the low point of a downtrend is called a dead cat bounce because the bounce isn't a live one. When it occurs on low volumes, it's called (rather disparagingly) a sucker rally because it's unlikely that professional traders participate in an apparent rally if the volume is low.

Tip

Check trade volumes when a trend first reverses and be wary if the reversal occurs on low volumes.

Minimising risk

Apart from checking volumes there are several strategies for minimising the risk of being whipsawed in a dead cat bounce or sucker rally. These strategies require the use of more advanced technical analysis techniques with indicators and filters.

I'll discuss them in later chapters, but for now I'll mention a simple strategy that doesn't require additional technical analysis. The idea is to use a time delay; that is, wait a number of trading days before acting on a trend change after it first appears. A typical time delay is three days; you delay taking any action for three trading days. After this time lapse you check the chart again, and if the trend still continues on reasonable volume you can trade with less risk of being whipsawed. The downside to this strategy is that you'll miss some of the profit available from the rising price because you won't be buying at a bargain basement price, so it boils down to balancing risk of loss against profit potential.

Tip

If you use a time delay before acting on an apparent trend change you reduce the risk of being whipsawed but you'll also lose some profit if the initial trend change is sustained.

Selling strategy

The question that now arises is: if I've bought in an uptrend, when should I sell?

I believe the best strategy is to sell after you're confident that the uptrend has changed to a downtrend. I've illustrated this strategy in figure 4.17.

Figure 4.17: uptrend selling strategy

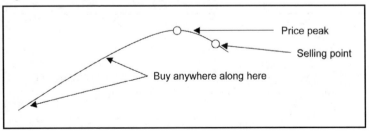

You might raise the following objection to this strategy: haven't I lost some profit—wouldn't it have been better to sell at the peak (or just before it) rather than waiting for the price to fall?

Clearly this objection is valid with the wisdom of hindsight. If you knew exactly when the price was going to peak you could sell right on the peak and maximise your profit. The problem is that you can't use the wisdom of hindsight in real time, and there's no way of knowing that a price has peaked until sometime afterward when the price has fallen back. It's simply impossible to predict a price peak in real time; you have to wait for the price to fall in order to know that a peak was reached.

Another advantage of my strategy is that frequently the pattern won't be an uptrend–downtrend one but rather an uptrend–sidetrend one. Then my strategy results in full profit because you can sell at your leisure and take full profits in the sidetrend, whereas if you'd sold in the uptrend before the peak was reached you'd make less profit. This situation is illustrated in figure 4.18.

Figure 4.18: selling in an uptrend–sidetrend pattern

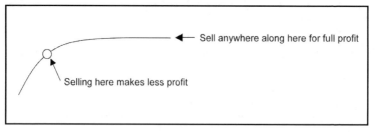

Tip

Don't sell in an uptrend. Ride the trend for as long as you can and sell only when the trend changes to a downtrend or sidetrend.

Wedge trading strategies

As I've said, it's best to avoid trading inside a wedge or triangle formation. If the wedge is a diverging one there's too much volatility with no clear trend, and if the wedge is a converging one the price range is reducing with little opportunity for significant profit. However, as I pointed out previously, an upward breakout from a converging wedge is usually a strong buy signal and a downward breakout a strong sell signal. The buy and sell points are illustrated in figure 4.19.

Figure 4.19: converging wedge — buy and sell points

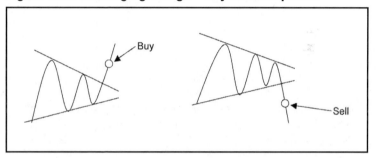

Tip

Buy on an upward breakout from a converging wedge and sell on a downward breakout.

Visual interpretation

I'll conclude this chapter by reiterating the subjective nature of visual chart interpretation. Some technical analysts try to make the interpretation less subjective using limiting parameters; for example, by defining a double top only when the two bounces occur within a specific time frame and are accompanied by certain volume changes. In my view there's no rational basis to these parameters, which add complexity without making the analysis more scientific.

As an example of subjectivity, how would you interpret the part of an OHLC chart shown in figure 4.20? (I've shown only the vertical bars in this diagram.)

Figure 4.20: OHLC chart bars

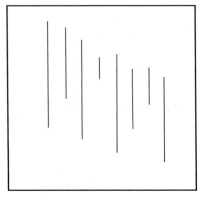

I came across this in a charting book and the author inferred a pattern of two converging triangles with downward breakout, as shown in figure 4.21.

Figure 4.21: converging triangles pattern

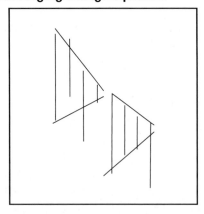

In this interpretation, the third bar from the left was regarded as abnormal and its drop below the triangle support was ignored.

When I saw the same bars I drew the conclusion that the pattern was one of a downward-sloping channel, as shown in figure 4.22.

Figure 4.22: downward channel pattern

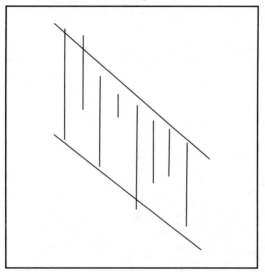

Which interpretation is correct? The reality is that there's no single correct interpretation. Like the interpretation of beauty, visual chart interpretation is in the eye of the beholder.

Tip

There's an element of subjectivity to pattern recognition; there's no precise interpretation.

Exercise

It's now time to try your hand at pattern recognition. I've reproduced a couple of charts on the following page that you can practise on and compare your interpretation with mine. They are both six-month OHLC charts from the CommSec site. Figure 4.23 is Lihir Gold (LHG) and figure 4.24 is OZ

Minerals (OZL). I've shown you my interpretation of these charts in the appendix (figures A4.23 and A4.24). If there are differences in your pattern interpretation to mine, don't be unduly alarmed; it's possible to come up with different patterns that are equally justifiable. We can produce different patterns and still both come up with a good result.

Figure 4.23: Lihir Gold

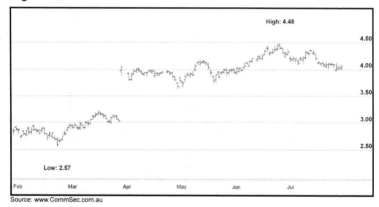

Source: www.CommSec.com.au

Figure 4.24: OZ Minerals

Source: www.CommSec.com.au

Tip

A good way to practise pattern recognition and fore-casting is to obtain a chart on the internet and quickly cover your computer screen with a thick sheet of paper before you've had a chance to interpret it. Gradually move the sheet over the screen from left to right and at each point ask yourself: is there a recognisable pattern, and what trading decision would I make at this point on the chart? If you have a partner or friend who's interested in technical analysis another good practice exercise is for each of you to analyse the same chart independently and then compare interpretations. In this way you can bounce ideas around and learn from one another.

Chapter summary

⇨ A pattern is a sequence of changes that recur frequently in charts. Recognising patterns helps you to forecast the most likely future scenario and improve your trading success.

⇨ The simplest pattern is a trend change from one of the three basic trends to another. The trend change can be sudden or a more gradual transition.

⇨ Long-term uptrends occur when the trend is due to sustainable earnings increases. Unsustainable uptrends based on wishful thinking (blue sky potential) are never long term and will inevitably correct downward (a retracement).

⇨ When shares go ex-dividend a sudden price drop will usually occur.

⇨ Sidetrends can last a long time, and require a change in sentiment to shake the price from its lethargic state. In a sidetrend breakout upward, the old resistance level often becomes a new support level, and in a downward move the old support level often becomes a new resistance level.

⇨ Downtrends can't be sustained over the long term because sooner or later the company will be taken over or declared bankrupt as the shares become virtually worthless.

⇨ Compound patterns form when there's a sequence of trend changes. The six most basic ones occur with two changes in each of the three basic trends.

⇨ The Fibonacci series can be used to derive ratios such as 0.38, 0.62, 1.38 and 1.62. Some analysts believe these ratios are significant and can be used to calculate trend turning points. Wave theory is based on the premise that share prices move in a sequence of waves according to the Fibonacci sequence.

⇨ The best time to buy into an uptrend is as soon as the uptrend occurs after a downtrend reversal or upward breakout from a sidetrend. However, if you act on the apparent trend reversal too soon you can be whipsawed, so it's a good idea to check volumes and make sure the apparent reversal isn't based on low volumes. You can also reduce the risk by building a time delay into your trading strategy.

⇨ Beware of sucker rallies and dead cat bounces as they result in whipsaw trades and losses.

⇨ In a strong uptrend the most reliable strategy is to ride the trend for as long as you can and sell only when the trend falters or reverses.

⇨ Converging wedge breakouts are usually significant. An upward breakout is often a reliable buy signal and a downward breakout a reliable sell signal.

⇨ Additional complexity won't necessarily improve your trading success.

⇨ Visual interpretation of a chart involves subjectivity; there's one single correct interpretation of a chart.

chapter 5

Moving averages

Moving averages are the most widely used indicators in technical analysis and are available on most websites with a charting facility. In this chapter I'll discuss the various types of moving average, how they're calculated and their advantages and limitations. I'll also suggest some suitable trading strategies you can use with moving averages.

The purpose of moving averages

A moving average helps you to distinguish an underlying trend within the fluctuations that occur as a result of day-to-day trading variations. Moving averages eliminate the subjectivity that's inevitable when you use the visual or 'eye' method to identify trends. The moving average trendline is calculated and shown on a chart according to the algorithm used by the charting software and the parameters you select. Moving averages are superimposed on the price chart so you're able to see prices and moving averages together.

The principle of moving averages

Suppose you're sailing and you want to know how the wind strength is changing so you can decide whether to reduce or increase sail area. You measure the wind speed on your indicator and the reading tells you the wind strength at that moment, but not how it's changing. To find this out you need to take at least one more reading some time later. When you do so you still won't have a reliable indication because the wind is seldom steady but blows in a series of alternating gusts and lulls. To get a more accurate diagnosis you need to obtain a set of readings, and later another set of readings, then average both sets and compare the two averages. Now you have a much more reliable indication of the wind strength trend because the average of a number of readings reduces the variation due to gusts.

The same principle applies to share prices, which fluctuate during the day and from day to day. This is normal in a free market where buyers and sellers compete, but these fluctuations muddy the waters when you're trying to identify price trends. To minimise their effect you need to average prices over some period, then average them out again in a later period and compare the averages. If the average is increasing this is a good indication of an underlying uptrend, if it's about the same then this indicates a sidetrend and if it's decreasing this indicates a downtrend.

To use the averaging principle to identify a trend it's necessary to average the same number of prices over different time periods. For example, in a 10-day moving average prices are averaged over the first 10 days, and in day 11 the day 11 price is added and the day 1 price is deleted. In day 12, the day 12 price is added and the day 2 price is deleted. In this way a 10-day moving average is obtained, and it's the average of the most recent 10 days of prices. Only one price can be used each day and by convention it's the closing price.

The number of days used for the moving average is known as the term. If you're using a weekly frequency for prices, the moving average will be based on weekly rather than daily closing prices.

Example 1

The method of calculating a moving average that I've outlined results in an average known as a simple moving average (SMA). I'll demonstrate the calculation using the closing price data given in table 5.1.

Table 5.1: SMA calculation

Day	1	2	3	4	5	6	7	8	9	10
Price	2.42	2.45	2.49	2.47	2.46	2.48	2.51	2.49	2.53	2.52
SMA	–	–	–	–	2.458	2.47	2.482	2.482	2.494	2.506

In this example I've calculated a 5-day moving average, so there's no average until day 5 because data is required for five days before the first moving average price can be calculated. The day 5 value is calculated as follows:

SMA (day 5) =
(2.42 + 2.45 + 2.49 + 2.47 + 2.46) ÷ 5 = 2.458

The day 6 SMA is calculated by adding the day 6 price and dropping off the day 1 price, as follows:

SMA (day 6) =
(2.45 + 2.49 + 2.47 + 2.46 + 2.48) ÷ 5 = 2.47

And so on.

Example 2

To simplify the calculation in the example I used a moving average term of five days. This is rather short, and you'll often want to use a longer term. Now I've calculated a 10-day SMA but this time I haven't shown you the calculation. Instead in figure 5.1 (overleaf) I've drawn a chart with these three lines:

⇨ closing prices shown as a line

⇨ trendline of best fit using the visual or 'eye' method

⇨ moving average.

Figure 5.1: prices, price trendline and 10-day SMA

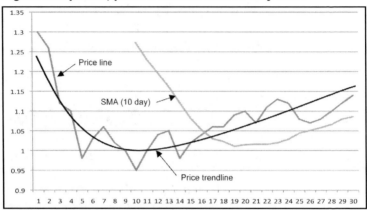

Source: Microsoft Excel screenshots used with permission from Microsoft.

Advantages of moving averages

This figure illustrates some of the advantages of moving averages:

⇨ A moving average smooths out the day-to-day price fluctuations and gives a better indication of the underlying trend than prices alone. When you use a moving average as a trend indicator (or change of trend indicator) you're less likely to be whipsawed.

⇨ The moving average trendline is drawn by the charting software so you don't need to exercise any judgement to identify a trend.

⇨ You can vary the term of the moving average in order to see short-term, medium-term and long-term trends.

⇨ A moving average can be used in conjunction with the price line to generate trading signals.

⇨ The charting software often allows you to call up two or more moving averages with different terms on the same chart. This provides some additional benefits and trading signals that I'll discuss later.

Limitations of moving averages

Figure 5.1 also demonstrates some of the limitations of moving averages:

⇨ When you're using a visual method to draw a trendline through a chart, you can use an OHLC chart (or variant of it such as the candle chart) and take into account the range of prices by joining the tops, bottoms or mid-points of the price bars. Only one data point in each time period can be used for a moving average and therefore some relevant trading data is excluded.

⇨ The moving average is a lagging indicator, which means that it lags price action. You can see from figure 5.1 that the first moving average point can't occur until day 10, by which time the day 1 price is 10 days old. To be in step with the price trend the moving average needs to be moved left (backward in time). The line of best fit I drew visually clearly shows a change in trend from downtrend to uptrend occurring around day 10, but the moving average doesn't indicate this trend change until about day 19. And the longer the term of the moving average, the greater the time lag.

Despite these limitations, moving averages are a very useful tool and are extensively used in technical analysis to identify trends and trend changes, and to generate trading signals as I'll outline later.

The time gap at the start of the moving average, as seen in the examples, won't be evident in most charts you look at because the shares will have been listed for some time. The moving average algorithm used by the charting software will go back in time to price data available before the first data point on the chart. Nevertheless, the time lag between the price trend and the moving average trend is still there and can't be avoided.

Even though a moving average is based on closing price only, a moving average can still be shown on an OHLC or candle chart.

Tip

Moving averages smooth day-to-day price variations and allow better identification of underlying trends. The trend identified by a moving average lags the price trend, and the longer the term of the moving average the greater the time lag.

Moving average time periods

When calling up a moving average you'll need to decide on the term. To help you make the decision, I'll provide some guidelines:

⇨ The term of the moving average should reflect the chart time period. For example, in a one-month chart there'd be no point in calling up a 20- or 30-day moving average. On the other hand, if you're looking at a 5-year chart, a 5- or 10-day moving average wouldn't be of much relevance; you'd want to use a longer one.

⇨ The term of the moving average should match the planned time frame of your trade. If you're planning for short-term trading profits you'll want to look at a short-term moving average. On the other hand, for a longer term investment you'll want to look at a medium to longer term moving average.

⇨ Try to balance the amount of smoothing and the time lag. The longer the moving average term, the smoother the line and the better the identification of the underlying trend. But the longer the term the greater the time lag before the moving average shows a trend change. Prices may have moved significantly by the time a long-term moving average shows a trend change, and much of your potential trading profit could have been eroded.

Tip

The time lag of a trend change indicated by a simple moving average is about half the term. For example, a 20-day SMA will lag a trend change by about 10 days.

Short- and long-term moving average comparison

Short-term and long-term moving averages are compared in table 5.2.

Table 5.2: advantages and disadvantages of short-term and long-term moving averages

	Advantages	Disadvantages
Short-term moving average	A trend change can be identified and acted on more quickly so you can trade at a better price and make more trading profit.	There's less smoothing so you have less confidence in the trend or trend change, so there's a greater likelihood of being whipsawed.
Long-term moving average	There's more smoothing so you have more confidence in the trend and trend changes, so there's less likelihood of being whipsawed.	A trend change can be identified and acted on less quickly so you may lose some of the price action and make less trading profit.

Suggested moving average terms

To provide some guidance, I suggest the moving average terms shown in table 5.3 (overleaf) according to the trend you're interested in.

Table 5.3: suggested moving average terms

Trend	Moving average term (days)
Short term	5 to 11
Medium term	13 to 31
Long term	50 to 250

In table 5.3 I assume a daily frequency, but if you're using a weekly frequency the moving average will be calculated using the closing price each week so the moving average term would be in weeks. The first row in table 5.3 wouldn't be relevant in this instance as you wouldn't be using a weekly chart to identify short-term trends.

Except for very short term moving averages you'll be hard pressed to notice any difference with a one- or two-day difference in the term. For example, there'll be little discernable difference between a 15-day and a 16-day moving average.

For the term of the moving average you can use odd numbers, even numbers, prime numbers, Fibonacci numbers or any other combination that suits the trade and gives the information you need.

Tip

Choose the term of your moving average to be consistent with the trend you're trying to identify.

Example 3

To demonstrate the difference between moving average terms I've reproduced a chart from the CommSec site with a 13-day and 50-day SMA (figure 5.2). This chart is for the Mona-delphous Group (MND) over a period of three years.

You can see that the 13-day moving average closely follows the price action and looks just like a line of best fit.

This is because over a period of three years a time lag of 13 days is hardly noticeable. The 50-day moving average smooths out the ripples and allows better identification of the longer term trend but the time lag is evident. The 50-day moving average appears as if it should be moved toward the left to more accurately reflect the price trend.

Figure 5.2: different term moving averages

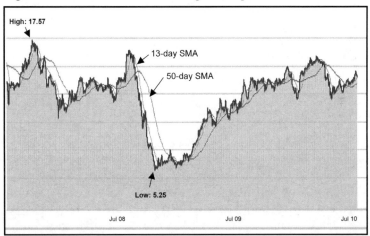

Source: www.CommSec.com.au

Note that when you call up two or more moving averages on the same chart they'll be different colours to make identification easier. All the diagrams and charts in this book are monochromatic so it won't be as easy to differentiate the lines, but you'll still be able to discriminate between different terms by the smoothness of the trendline and the amount of time lag.

Exponential moving averages

To minimise the time-lag problem and make a moving average more sensitive to current price action, most charting software provides a moving average that's weighted according to an exponential algorithm. I won't quote the formula (it's rather complex); instead in figure 5.3 (overleaf) I've shown the weighting factors produced by an exponential curve.

This produces what is known as an exponential moving average (EMA).

Figure 5.3: exponential weighting factors

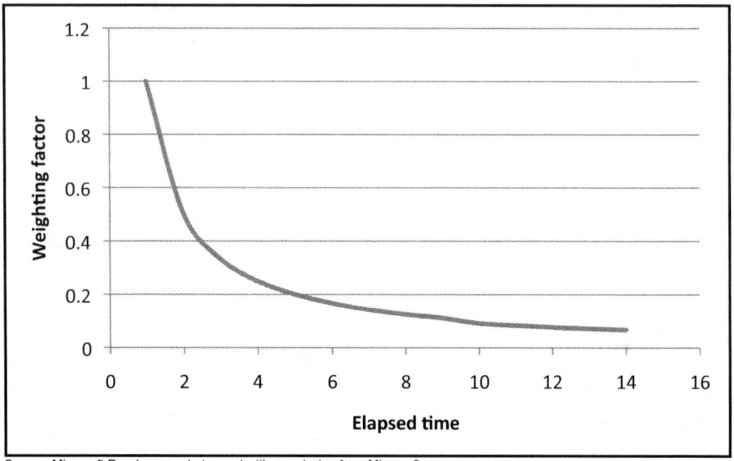

Source: Microsoft Excel screenshots used with permission from Microsoft.

The weighting factor steadily reduces as the elapsed time increases, so less weight is given to older prices than to more recent ones. This makes the EMA more sensitive and allows you to detect a price trend change with less time lag than the SMA. This can be significant with shorter term moving averages but is less noticeable with longer term ones. In the EMA calculation (unlike the SMA) old prices don't actually drop out, they just decay exponentially and eventually become insignificant.

Tip

The EMA allows you to detect trend changes with less time lag than the SMA.

Weighted moving averages

Some charting software provides a third type of moving average: a weighted moving average (WMA). Like the EMA it's more sensitive to recent data, so trend changes can be detected more rapidly. In the WMA a weighting factor is used that gives more weight to recent prices and less weight to older prices according to an algorithm. A typical weighting method is to use the sum of the time period method. As a simple example, consider a five-day moving average. The numbers 1 to 5 add to 15 (1 + 2 + 3 + 4 + 5 = 15), and using this method the weighting factors are as shown in table 5.4.

Table 5.4: five-day weighting factors

Elapsed time (days)	1	2	3	4	5
Weighting factor	5/15	4/15	3/15	2/15	1/15

Using these weighting factors, the most recent price is given five times more weight than the price five days ago.

The WMA algorithm differs from the EMA algorithm in a key aspect: old prices drop out of the WMA each new day rather than decaying exponentially. For example, with a five-day WMA, on day 6 the price from day 1 is eliminated.

Example 4

To illustrate the difference between the various moving averages, I've provided a chart (from the CommSec site) for the same company as I used in figure 5.2 (Monadelphous Group), but this time over a shorter time period with a 13-day moving average of each type (figure 5.4, overleaf).

You can see that there's a small difference between the three moving averages, but the difference isn't nearly as significant as you might expect from the very different algorithms used. With medium- to long-term moving averages there's little difference between the three. The difference becomes more noticeable when using short-term moving averages; the EMA and the WMA will clearly indicate the trend change before the SMA. The WMA is usually a little more sensitive to a trend change than the EMA. While the EMA is usually available with most charting software, the WMA is less widely provided.

Figure 5.4: SMA, EMA and WMA compared

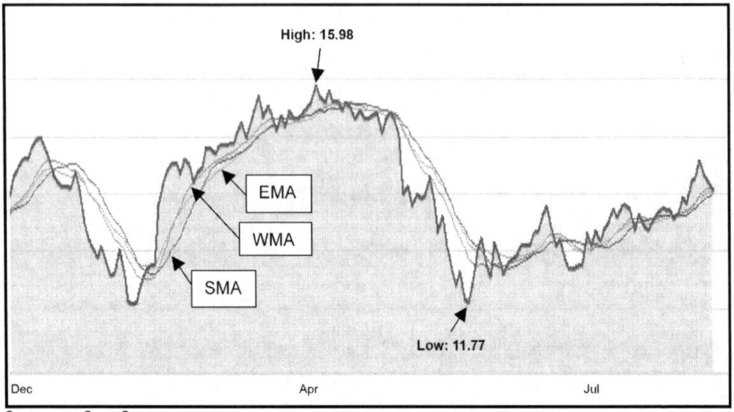

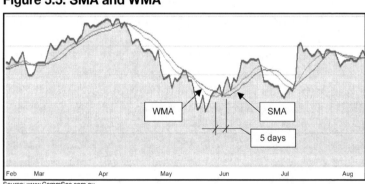

Source: www.CommSec.com.au

Example 5

To show you the difference between trend changes indicated by the SMA and WMA more clearly, I've provided a chart with a 13-day SMA and 13-day WMA. This chart (from the CommSec site) is shown as figure 5.5, and it's for Santos (STO) over a six-month period. I've expanded the chart vertically for clearer visual impact.

Figure 5.5: SMA and WMA

Source: www.CommSec.com.au

You can see the change from downtrend to uptrend in June that's indicated about five days earlier with the WMA than with the SMA. For short-term trading, this could be a significant advantage.

Tip

Investigate the moving averages available with the charting software you're using and experiment with them. If the WMA is available I suggest you use it as it's usually the most sensitive to trend changes. If it's not available the EMA is the next best choice.

Example 6

As I said previously, even though a moving average is calculated using closing prices only there's no reason why you can't use moving averages on an OHLC chart or candle chart. As an example I've reproduced figure 5.5 as an OHLC chart, as shown in figure 5.6. This chart is from the CommSec site and includes volume.

Figure 5.6: OHLC chart with SMA and WMA

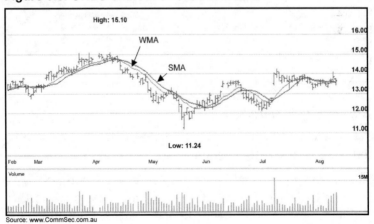

Source: www.CommSec.com.au

Single moving average strategies

I'll now outline some trading strategies you can use with moving averages. They're based on the same principles I've outlined previously in chapters 3 and 4, and that I'll now summarise:

⇨ The trend is your friend. Buy (go long) in an uptrend. Don't buy in a downtrend, sell if you are currently holding or go short.

⇨ Trend changes are usually good trading signals, and there's potential for the most profit if you act quickly. At the same time you need to exercise caution to avoid being whipsawed or getting your fingers burnt in a sucker rally or dead cat bounce.

The basic strategies using a moving average are illustrated in figure 5.7. In this diagram I've indicated the probable future moving average trend using a dashed line.

Figure 5.7: moving average trading strategies

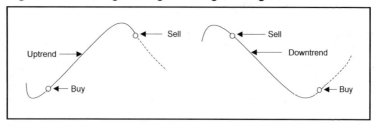

Charting parameters

When using moving averages you need to decide on the following four charting parameters:

⇨ The time period and frequency of the chart. Are you going to look at a chart for today (intra-day) or a short, intermediate or long time period chart? Are you going to use a daily, weekly or even monthly frequency?

⇨ Which type of chart are you going to use? With a single moving average I suggest you use an OHLC or candle chart for shorter time periods and a line chart for longer time periods.

⇨ Which moving average are you going to use? I suggest you call up a WMA or EMA, but an SMA is also okay, especially for longer term trends.

⇨ The term of the moving average — will you call up a short-term, medium-term or long-term one?

Tip

Experiment with the four charting parameters I've outlined and determine your own preferences.

You can show moving averages and prices on the same chart, so you can use strategies based on them as follows:

⇨ *Strong uptrend:* both price and moving average trend upward with prices consistently above the moving average.

⇨ *Strong downtrend:* both price and moving average trend downward with prices consistently below the moving average.

⇨ *Buy signal:* the price crosses upward above the moving average. This is known as a price golden cross.

⇨ *Sell signal:* the prices crosses downward below the moving average. This is known as a price dead cross.

These strategies are illustrated in figure 5.8 (overleaf). Note that you can't use these strategies in a sidetrend.

These strategies are most effective with a medium to longer term moving average, and you need to exercise caution if the moving average is a short-term one. A short-term moving average closely follows the price action so the price and moving average will often cross one another. If you use the crossovers as trading signals you risk frequent whipsaws.

Figure 5.8: price and single moving average strategies

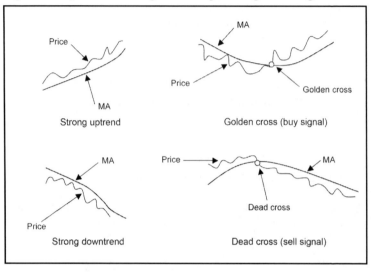

In figure 5.8 I show prices as a line chart. You can also use an OHLC or candle chart but then price bars may frequently cross the moving average, making it more difficult to identify significant crossover points. For this reason, I prefer to use the line chart when identifying golden and dead crosses with a single moving average.

Tip

Moving average golden and dead crosses are powerful trading signals and are best identified with a price line chart.

Example 7

I'll now illustrate these strategies with a chart (figure 5.9). It's a line chart for Santos from the CommSec site, and it's essentially the same as figure 5.5 except that now I've shown one moving average only and it's a 13-day EMA (low end of the medium-term range).

Figure 5.9: line (mountain) chart with 13-day EMA

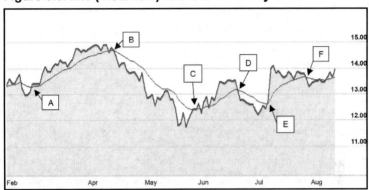

Source: www.CommSec.com.au

I've marked points A to F on the chart. The significant features and trading signals are:

⇨ A: golden cross—buy at $13.40

⇨ A to B: strong uptrend—the price line is consistently above the EMA

⇨ B: dead cross—sell at $14.70

⇨ B to C: strong downtrend—the price line is consistently below the EMA

⇨ C: golden cross—buy at $12.50. You can see that the price line seesaws above and below the moving average line briefly after this point and would result in whipsaws if you treated each one as a trading signal and acted immediately

⇨ C to D: brief uptrend

⇨ D: dead cross—sell at $13.10

⇨ D to E: brief downtrend

⇨ E: golden cross—buy at $12.70

⇨ E to F: brief uptrend

⇨ F: dead cross—sell at $13.60.

Example 8

I've calculated the trading profit using the trading signals identified in example 7, assuming $10 000 invested at each buy point and a $20 brokerage cost. The results are shown in table 5.5.

Table 5.5: trades and profit

	Number of shares purchased	$ selling revenue	$ profit
A to B	745	10 931	931
C to D	798	10 434	434
E to F	786	10 669	669
Total profit			**2034**

The percentage return is 20.34% in six months, which is an annualised return on capital of 40.7%. Actually, because most of the trades were of fairly short duration, the total time trading capital was tied up in these trades was about half that so the annualised return on capital is more like about 80%. In real-time trading you may not be able to trade at the precise crossover price but the example illustrates the potential benefits of using moving average trading signals.

Tip

You can make good profits by acting on price and moving average crossover trading signals, but it's necessary to strike a balance between acting too quickly and risking a whipsaw and delaying action and missing some potential profit.

Example 9

In example 7 I used a line chart. Just to point out the difference, I'll show you the same chart except that prices are shown in OHLC format. This chart is shown as figure 5.10.

Figure 5.10: OHLC chart with 13-day EMA

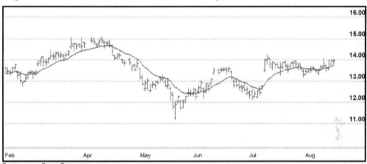

Source: www.CommSec.com.au

You can see that with an OHLC chart precise crossover points are more difficult to identify. However, this chart shows additional information, including the gaps, so you may prefer to use it rather than the line chart. It's really a matter of personal preference.

Two moving average strategies

Most charting software allows you to chart more than one moving average simultaneously so you can add a tier of refinement to the moving average trading strategies I've outlined by using a shorter term average in conjunction with a longer term one. (I use the terminology shorter term and longer term here rather than short term and long term because the suggested time periods aren't the same as those in table 5.3.)

As a rule of thumb, the longer average should be about three times the shorter one. It's a matter of personal choice and experimentation, but as a starting point I suggest moving average terms for various time frames, as shown in table 5.6 (overleaf).

Table 5.6: shorter and longer moving average terms

Trend time frame	Shorter term MA (days)	Longer term MA (days)
Short	5	17
Medium	13	50
Long	31	100

Some traders use moving average terms that are Fibonacci numbers, chosen from the series 5, 8, 13, 21, 34, 55, 89, 144, 233, and so on. Adopting this system, you could use 5 and 13, 13 and 34, and 34 and 144 for the shorter, medium and longer terms respectively, but I see no logical rationale for doing so.

Because the shorter moving average reacts more quickly to trend changes than the longer one, similar strategies can be derived with two moving averages as I outlined previously. The crossover trading signal is more reliable but there'll be more time lag. The strategies are:

⇨ *Strong uptrend:* both moving averages trend upward with the shorter moving average consistently above the longer one.

⇨ *Strong downtrend:* both moving averages trend downward with the shorter moving average consistently below the longer one.

⇨ *Buy signal:* the shorter moving average trends upward and crosses above the longer one. This is a moving average golden cross.

⇨ *Sell signal:* the shorter moving average trends downward and crosses below the longer one. This is a moving average dead cross.

As before, in a sidetrend these strategies can't be applied. These strategies are illustrated in figure 5.11. Here I use STMA to denote the shorter term moving average and LTMA to indicate the longer term one, which is shown with a thicker line.

Figure 5.11: shorter term and longer term moving average strategies

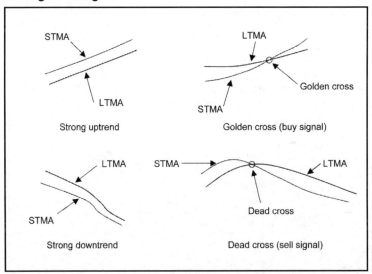

Tip

Moving average crossovers indicate a trend change and can be used as trading signals. The signals are usually more reliable than the price and moving average crossover signal but involve more time lag.

Example 10

Figure 5.12 (overleaf) is a three-year chart for Commonwealth Bank (CBA) from the CommSec site showing 31- and 100-day EMAs. I've marked the crossover points with the letters A, B and C.

The following are shown:

⇨ A: dead cross, signalling trend reversal from uptrend to downtrend.

⇨ A to B: strong downtrend to sidetrend and downtrend again with the shorter moving average remaining below the longer one even during the sidetrend.

⇨ B: golden cross, signalling the downtrend reversal.

⇨ B to C: strong uptrend with shorter moving average consistently above the longer one.

⇨ C: dead cross, signalling the end of the long uptrend.

Figure 5.12: line (mountain) chart with 31- and 100-day EMAs

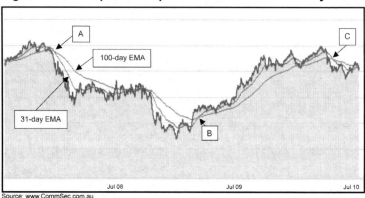

Source: www.CommSec.com.au

Price and two moving average strategies

A line chart with two moving averages has three lines that can cross one another. So there are three crossover points that can be used to identify a golden or dead cross:

⇨ price crosses the shorter moving average (shown as (a) in figure 5.13)

⇨ price crosses the longer moving average (shown as (b))

⇨ shorter moving average crosses the longer moving average (shown as (c)).

I've illustrated these crossover points for a golden cross in figure 5.13, but these crossover points can also be used to identify a dead cross.

Figure 5.13: crossover points for a golden cross

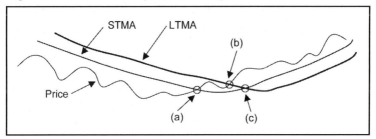

Choice of crossover points

Which of these crossover points you'll use as a trading signal depends upon the planned time frame of the trade and your risk profile. As a guide, the relative advantages and disadvantages and suitability of each are outlined in table 5.7.

Table 5.7: crossover points advantages, disadvantages and suitability

Crossover point	Advantage	Disadvantage	Suitability
(a)	Fastest response/ shortest time lag. You can trade at the best price.	Highest risk of whipsaw.	Short-term trades for higher risk traders.
(c)	Lowest risk of whipsaw.	Slowest response/ longest time lag. Prices may have moved significantly by the time you respond.	Longer term trades for lower risk traders.
(b)	In between (a) and (c).	In between (a) and (c).	Medium-term trades for medium-risk traders.

You can use crossover point (a) with longer term trades by using it as an alert signal rather than a trading signal, indicating that a trend change could be imminent. This is especially useful with dead crosses, and as soon as crossover (a) appears you need to follow the market closely as it's a warning signal that a downtrend reversal is likely.

Tip

With long- or medium-term trades it's safest to use the moving average crossover points as trade signals, but price crossover points can still be used as alert signals.

Short-term trading signals

In example 10 I used longer term moving averages with a long-term chart and this is the safest option for long-term traders or investors. For short-term trading you'll be using a shorter time period chart and moving average terms. You can then use crossovers as warning or trade signals as follows:

⇨ price and longer moving average crossover: warning signal of a trend change (this can also be used as a trading signal but may result in frequent whipsaws)

⇨ shorter and longer moving average crossover: good indication of a trend change and a good trading signal.

Example 11

As an example of short-term trading signals consider figure 5.14.

Figure 5.14: line chart with 12-day and 31-day EMAs

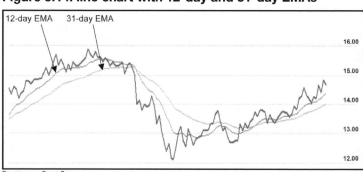

Source: www.CommSec.com.au

It's a six-month line chart taken from the CommSec site for Monadelphous, showing the 12-day and 31-day EMAs. Try to identify the crossovers and signals and check them with my interpretation given in appendix figure A5.14.

Multiple moving averages

Some charting software provides for more than two moving averages. Some chartists chart up to 10 moving averages simultaneously, but I feel that this is adding too much complexity without appreciable benefit. I suggest you use no more than three moving averages with short-, medium- and long-term periods from the range I suggested in table 5.6. You will have additional crossover points, and you'll need to decide which of these to use as warning or trading signals.

Multiple averages with OHLC or candle charts

An OHLC or candle chart provides useful information not available with a line chart, but as I pointed out before, the problem with these charts is that the price bars often cross the moving average and muddy the waters when you're trying to identify crossover points. A way of overcoming this disadvantage is to make one of the moving averages a very short one; for example, five days. Then you can treat this moving average as a line of best fit and use it in conjunction with 12-day and 31-day moving averages as before.

Tip

Use a very short term moving average with an OHLC or candle chart and treat it as a price trendline.

Example 12

An example of an OHLC chart with three moving averages is shown in figure 5.15 (overleaf). This chart (taken from the Incredible Charts site) is the same chart as figure 5.14

(Monadelphous, six months) except that now I've included the 5-day EMA in addition to the 12-day and 31-day averages. You can now see several gaps in the chart that weren't apparent in figure 5.14.

Figure 5.15: OHLC chart with 5-day, 12-day and 31-day EMAs

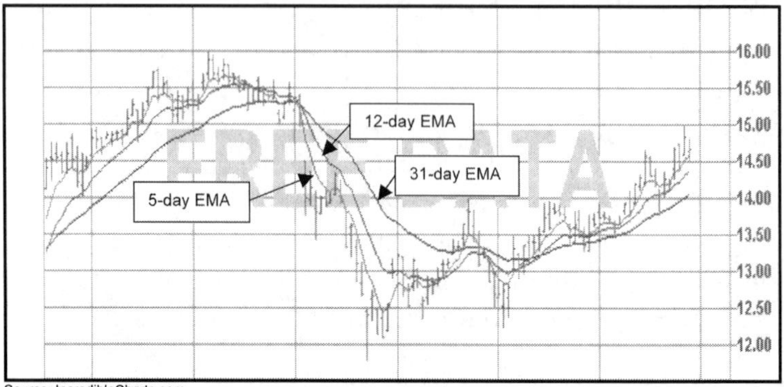

Source: IncredibleCharts.com

Tip

Examine charts of interest to you and experiment with different types of moving averages, terms, time periods and chart formats. Identify trend changes and trading signals and decide on your preferences.

Chapter summary

⇨ Moving averages allow you to distinguish objectively between price ripples and underlying trends.

⇨ Moving averages eliminate the subjectivity that's inevitable with the visual or 'eye' method to identify trends or patterns and changes in trend.

⇨ A moving average is a lagging indicator as there's a time delay between a price trend change and the moving average trend change. This disadvantage is offset by the advantage that a moving average is a more reliable trend change indicator than price alone.

⇨ There are three main types of moving average used in charting: simple moving average (SMA), exponential moving average (EMA) and weighted moving average (WMA).

⇨ The SMA is the average closing price over a number of days with each price given equal weight, whereas EMAs and WMAs give more weight to recent prices and less to earlier prices. Therefore they're more sensitive to trend changes and they detect them earlier than the SMA.

⇨ The time period of a moving average should match the time frame of your planned trade or investment.

⇨ Crossover points between the price and moving average can be used to generate trading signals. A buy signal is known as a golden cross and a sell signal as a dead cross.

⇨ Moving average crossovers are best used with uptrends or downtrends but don't apply in sidetrends.

⇨ You can show a moving average on a line chart, OHLC chart or candle chart, but for identifying crossover points with a single moving average it's easiest to use a line chart.

⇨ Most charting software allows you to call up more than one moving average on the same chart. Crossovers between the two moving averages can be used to identify golden and dead crosses.

⇨ With two moving averages use a shorter term and a longer term one. The longer term one is usually about three times the shorter one.

⇨ Two moving averages in conjunction with prices can produce three crossover points: price and shorter MA, price and longer MA, and shorter and longer MA. The choice of which one you'll use depends upon your risk profile and the planned time frame of your trade.

⇨ Three moving averages provide an additional tier of refinement that you can experiment with once you become proficient at using two.

⇨ For relatively short term trading with three moving averages, use a very short term average (about five days) as well as longer ones such as 12 days and 31 days. The 5-day moving average is equivalent to a price line of best fit (on an OHLC or candle chart) whereas the 12-day and 31-day crossover identify golden and dead cross trading signals.

chapter 6

Moving average convergence divergence

In chapter 5 I discussed the most widely used tool in charting: the moving average indicator. One or more moving averages used in conjunction with visual trend interpretation are the backbone of technical analysis and provide a sound platform for strategic decision-making. To refine your analysis there are other tools you can use, and the most important of these is the moving average convergence divergence indicator, abbreviated to MACD. In this chapter I'll describe how it's calculated and how you can use it to improve your technical analysis.

Moving average difference

The MACD indicator is based on moving averages but provides some additional indications that can help to refine your analysis. To understand the principle of the MACD consider figure 6.1 (overleaf).

Figure 6.1: moving average difference

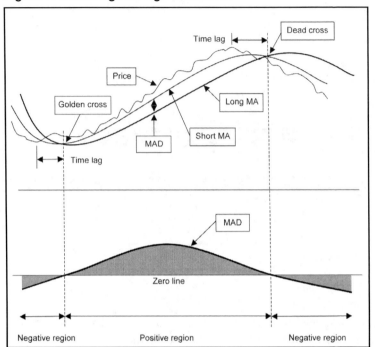

This diagram illustrates a typical price wave sequence with the price changing from downtrend to uptrend and back to downtrend again. I've shown two moving averages: a shorter term one (thinner line) and a longer term one (thicker line), and I've marked the moving average golden cross and dead cross crossover signals. You can see that there's a time lag between the price trend change and the moving average crossover, which I've also marked on the diagram.

If you examine the separation between the two moving averages, you can see that there's an indication of a trend change some time before the crossover point. At the left side of the diagram the moving averages converge as the downtrend falters and then cross—a golden cross buy signal. After the crossover they diverge as the uptrend gathers pace, then converge again as the uptrend falters until they give a dead cross sell signal. After the crossover they diverge again as the downtrend gathers pace.

I've shown the separation (or difference) between the two moving averages as a separate line marked MAD—moving average difference—at the bottom of figure 6.1. The line will be above the axis (positive) if the short MA is above the long MA, and below the axis (negative) if the short MA is below the long MA.

The trend indications from the moving average difference are:

⇨ strong uptrend: short MA is above the long MA and difference is positive

⇨ strong downtrend: short MA is below the long MA and difference is negative.

The slope of the moving average difference line also provides an indication of a pending trend change. You can see that the moving average difference line peaked and then started to downtrend even though the uptrend was still in progress; this indicates that the uptrend is faltering.

In summary, the two important questions with the moving average difference are:

⇨ Is the difference positive or negative?

⇨ Is the difference line sloping upward or downward?

Tip

The greater the moving average difference the stronger the trend, and a change in the slope of the moving average difference indicates a likely trend change.

The MACD indicator

I've outlined the principles on which the MACD indicator is based. This indicator is calculated using two exponential moving averages; by default 12-day and 26-day EMAs are usually used. The difference between them is calculated and charted as a line known as the MACD line, and this line will appear the same as the moving average difference line at the bottom of figure 6.1. Now comes the cunning part — the MACD line is exponentially smoothed; that's to say, it's treated just like a price line, and a nine-day exponential moving average of it is calculated and shown as another line known as the signal line. Because the signal line is an exponential moving average of the MACD line it will lag the MACD line, so when both are charted they will appear very similar to short and long moving averages.

Because the MACD line is the difference between the 12-day and 26-day EMAs it can be positive or negative depending upon whether the 12-day EMA line is above or below the 26-day EMA line. If the 12-day EMA is above the 26-day it will be positive, and if the 12-day EMA is below the 26-day it will be negative.

In summary:

⇨ The MACD line and signal line can be above or below zero (positive or negative).

⇨ The MACD line and signal line can cross each other above or below the zero axis.

The MACD line is also known as the fast line and the signal line as the slow line (for obvious reasons). The MACD line and signal line are charted using different colours to make identification easier.

Tip

It will help you to distinguish between the MACD line and the signal line if you remember that the signal line is smoothed and therefore appears as a smoother line than the MACD line, which is more undulating.

The MACD histogram

As we've seen in chapter 5, moving averages are shown on the price chart which makes them easy to visually interpret. However, the MACD indicator is shown as an additional chart below the price chart, and if a volume chart is also provided vertical space becomes a problem. The MACD chart will be relatively small, making it difficult to clearly identify the crossover points between the MACD line and the signal line.

Most charting software mitigates this problem by showing the difference between the MACD line and the signal line as a bar chart — also known as a histogram. The histogram shows the difference between the MACD line and the signal line and so will move up and down across the zero axis. The bars will be above zero (positive) when the MACD line is above the signal line and below zero (negative) when the MACD line is below the signal line. This makes the crossover points between the MACD line and the signal line much easier to identify because they occur when the histogram bar length is zero — the bars cross the zero axis.

Tip

Zero bars on the MACD histogram allow you to clearly identify crossover points between the MACD line and the signal line.

Example 1

Figure 6.2 (overleaf) is a six-month OHLC chart (taken from the CommSec site) for Santos (STO) showing the 13-day EMA, and is the same chart used in chapter 5 (figure 5.10) except that it now shows the MACD. Because CommSec charts tend to be squashed vertically, I omitted the volume chart and expanded the chart in the vertical direction to show the MACD lines more clearly.

Figure 6.2: OHLC, MA and MACD

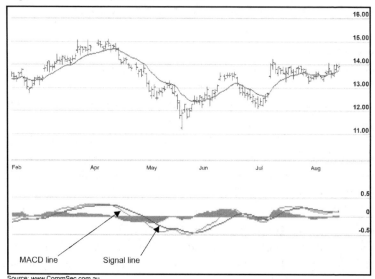

Source: www.CommSec.com.au

I've marked the MACD line and the signal line, and you can see that they converge and diverge and cross over (both above and below zero). You can also see that the MACD histogram allows you to better identify the crossover points.

Tip

The Incredible Charts site provides more vertical space in their charts and this makes their charts easier to visually interpret.

MACD trading strategies

Crossovers between the MACD line and signal line can be used to generate trading signals in virtually the same way as moving average crossovers. However, they frequently cross one another, and if you trade on each crossover you can often be whipsawed.

The risk of whipsaws can be minimised by adopting the following strategies:

⇨ Buy (go long) when the MACD line crosses above the signal line and both are below zero. This is an MACD golden cross (similar to a moving average golden cross).

⇨ Sell (or go short) when the MACD crosses below the signal line and both are above zero. This is an MACD dead cross (similar to a moving average dead cross).

These strategies are illustrated in figure 6.3.

Figure 6.3: MACD crossovers

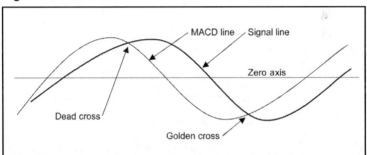

These strategies are based on the following principles:

⇨ When the MACD line crosses above the signal line (golden cross) and the crossover occurs when both are negative, the most likely price move is upward.

⇨ When the MACD line crosses below the signal line (dead cross) and the crossover occurs when both are positive, the most likely price move is downward.

These strategies minimise the risk of whipsaws and are most reliable when the crossover occurs well above or below the zero axis. The closer the crossover is to the zero axis, the less reliable the indication.

Cautionary signals

When the MACD line crosses below the signal line and both are below the zero axis, this isn't a true MACD dead cross (according to the stated strategies). However, I suggest you regard it as a cautionary signal of a downtrend change, especially if there's also price weakness.

Tip

The MACD crossover trading strategies I've outlined provide generally reliable trading signals and minimise the risk of whipsaws. However, they're most reliable when the crossover occurs well above or below the zero line.

Histogram trend indications

The histogram can be used as a trend indicator as follows:

⇨ The bars are principally above zero in an uptrend and below zero in a downtrend.

⇨ The length of the bars gives an indication of the strength of the trend. Long bars indicate a strong trend, and the shortening of the bars indicates the trend is faltering. This is seen in a change in slope of the bars. For example, a change from an upslope to a downslope indicates a faltering uptrend, and a change from a downslope to an upslope indicates an impending trend change from downtrend to uptrend.

These indications are illustrated in figure 6.4.

Tip

Changes in the slope of the MACD histogram bars provide a warning of a faltering trend, but the change may not eventuate for some time. For example, in an uptrend the upslope may change to a downslope but the uptrend can also continue for a considerable time after the change occurs.

Figure 6.4: histogram bar slopes

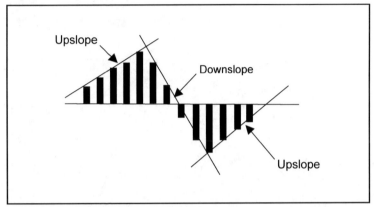

MACD time lag

The strength of a moving average derives from its ability to identify an underlying trend from the day-to-day trading price fluctuations. However, this strength is also a source of weakness because the moving average is a lagging indicator and the longer the term of the moving average the greater the time lag. When there's a strongly established trend this time lag isn't of great significance, but it's more troublesome when there's a change in trend because the trend change won't be signalled until some time after it's occurred. Naturally you want to trade at the best price, and if you don't trade until the moving average indicates a trend change you can miss some of the profit made by traders who act more promptly.

Somewhat paradoxically, the MACD indicator crossover signal usually occurs prior to the moving average crossover signal—that's to say, there's less time lag—and this is an important advantage.

Example 2

Let's now look at a chart and identify the trading signals indicated by moving averages and the MACD. The OHLC chart in figure 6.5 is for Bluescope Steel (BSL) for a time period of six months taken from the Incredible Charts site, showing the 5-day, 12-day and 31-day EMAs. The MACD chart with histogram is shown below the price chart, and I've expanded it vertically to make it easier to interpret.

Figure 6.5: OHLC chart with MACD

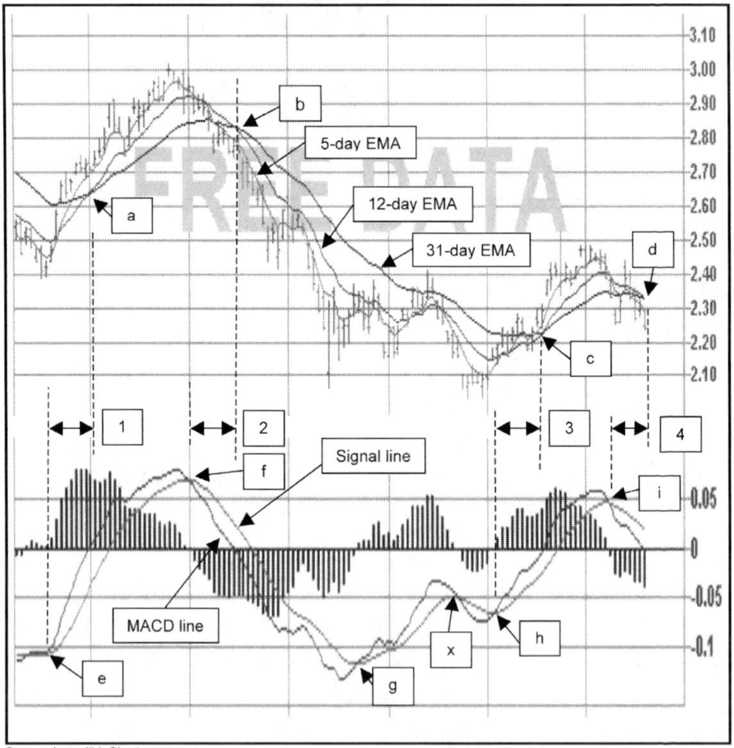

Source: IncredibleCharts.com

Because the price chart is in OHLC format, I'll use the 5-day EMA as a trend indicator. I've marked the crossovers between the 12-day and 31-day EMAs with the letters 'a' to 'd'.

The moving average crossover trading signals are:

⇨ a: golden cross: 12-day EMA crosses above 31-day EMA

⇨ b: dead cross: 12-day EMA crosses below 31-day EMA

⇨ c: golden cross: 12-day EMA crosses above 31-day EMA

⇨ d: dead cross: 12-day EMA crosses below 31-day EMA.

The MACD crossover trading signals are marked with the letters 'e' to 'i' and are:

⇨ e: golden cross: MACD line crosses above signal line and both are below zero

⇨ f: dead cross: MACD line crosses below signal line and both are above zero

⇨ g: golden cross: MACD line crosses above signal line and both are below zero

⇨ h: golden cross: MACD line crosses above signal line and both are below zero

⇨ i: dead cross: MACD line crosses below signal line and both are above zero.

Point 'x' is a crossover that appears to be a dead cross but isn't one according to the trading strategies I suggested because the crossover occurs below zero and not above it.

In figure 6.5 you can see the indications given by the histogram and how the bars crossing the zero axis clearly identify MACD crossovers. You will note that around point 'a' the histogram bars change slope and start to downtrend, warning that the uptrend is losing strength, but the price downtrend didn't occur until a considerable time later.

Crossover time lags

I've marked the time lag differences between the moving average and MACD crossovers with the numbers 1 to 4 in figure 6.5, and you can see that in each case the MACD crossover occurs prior to the moving average crossover. This demonstrates the benefit of using MACD crossovers to identify golden and dead cross trading signals because there's less time lag.

Tip

MACD crossovers usually alert you to probable trend changes more rapidly than moving average crossovers.

Example 3

Figure 6.6 is a line chart from the Incredible Charts site that I've expanded vertically. It's for Bank of Queensland (BOQ) with 13-day and 31-day EMAs shown. Below the price chart the MACD lines and histogram are charted.

Figure 6.6: line chart with MACD

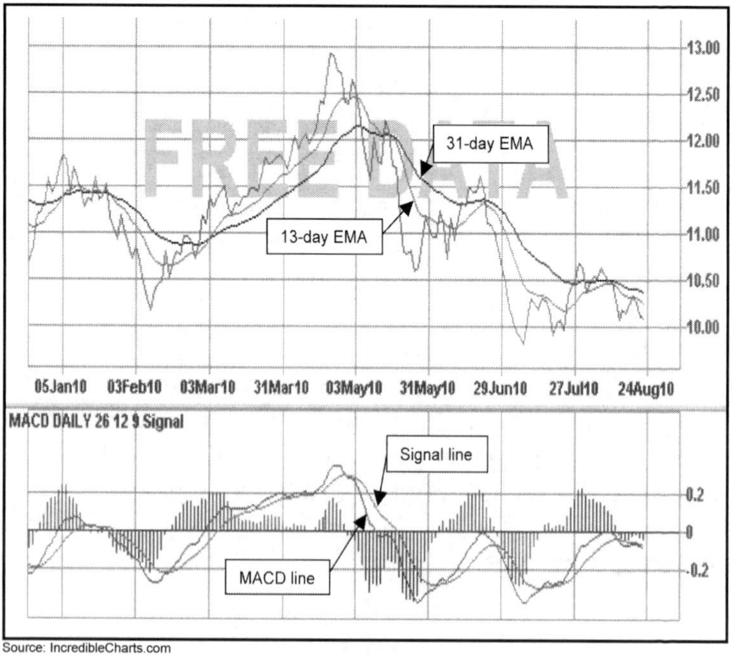

Source: IncredibleCharts.com

As an exercise, try your hand at identifying trading signals using both moving average and MACD crossovers. My interpretation is given in appendix figure A6.6.

Using the MACD

The MACD is a useful indicator when used in conjunction with visual chart inspection and moving averages. I suggest you don't use MACD signals in isolation but as confirmation of trends or trend changes. If the MACD confirms the price trend and moving average indications this increases your confidence, but if there's a contrary indication it's a divergence that flashes a warning that further investigation is required.

MACD signals are most valuable when a strong trend is faltering and a change of trend is likely. When a downtrend is weakening and a change to uptrend is commencing it's the best time to buy. MACD signals also alert you to times when you should consider selling if you've bought into an uptrend that's weakening. The MACD has little value in sidetrends because there'll be too many crossovers close to the zero axis and these won't provide sufficiently reliable signals. I find the MACD to be most useful with charts where the time period is six months or less. Over longer time periods there are usually frequent crossovers that tend to muddy the waters rather than providing useful indications.

Tip

Don't use the MACD indicator in isolation but use it in conjunction with visual trend analysis and moving averages. It's most useful in relatively short term charts.

Practise your identification

I suggest you practise using the MACD indicator on the charting website of your choice. Identify crossovers and trading signals using both MACD and moving averages and assess the reliability of the indications.

Chapter summary

⇨ MACD stands for moving average convergence divergence, and (as the name suggests) the basic principle underlying the indicator is the difference between two moving averages.

⇨ The MACD is conventionally calculated using 12-day and 26-day exponential moving averages and charted as the MACD line (sometimes called the fast line).

⇨ A nine-day EMA of the MACD is calculated and charted as a line known as the signal line (sometimes called the slow line). As you'd expect the signal line is smoother than the MACD line (just as an EMA line is smoother that the price line from which it's derived).

⇨ The difference between the MACD line and the signal line is significant and it's usually charted as a bar chart, known as the MACD histogram.

⇨ The MACD line, signal line and histogram are usually shown as a separate chart below the price and volume chart.

⇨ If the MACD line is above the signal line the difference is positive and the histogram bars are above zero. If the MACD line is below the signal line the difference is negative and the histogram bars are below zero.

⇨ The MACD line and signal line frequently cross above or below the zero axis. When they cross, the histogram bars have no height because the difference is zero.

⇨ Crossover points between the MACD line and signal line provide trading signals in a similar way to short and long moving average crossovers. An MACD golden cross (buy signal) occurs when the MACD line crosses above the signal line and both are below zero, and an MACD dead cross (sell signal) occurs when the MACD line crosses below the signal line and both are above zero.

⇨ The further away from the zero axis the crossover occurs, the more reliable the signal.

⇨ When the MACD line crosses below the signal line and both are below zero it's not a trading signal but a cautionary one, especially if there's also price weakness.

⇨ The MACD shouldn't be used in isolation to provide trading signals but is most useful when considered in conjunction with visual trend identification and moving averages.

⇨ The MACD indicator is most useful for relatively short time periods (less than one year) as a longer term chart will usually have too many crossovers to be useful.

chapter 7

Momentum

In this chapter I'll look at momentum in the market and its significance to share trading. I'll describe the momentum indicator as a way of measuring momentum and the advantages and limitations of this indicator.

Physical momentum

Momentum in the physical world stems from Newton's first law of motion which states that a body will remain at rest or in uniform motion unless a force acts on it to change that state. If you place a book on a table the law implies that the book will stay there forever unless a force acts on it and causes it to move. On the other hand, a moving body will keep moving forever in the same way unless a force acts on it to speed it up, slow it down or stop it.

Sharemarket momentum

No doubt you're wondering what relevance physical momentum has to the sharemarket. The connection comes about because share prices appear to exhibit momentum and obey Newton's law in a similar way to a physical body. Like a physical body, price resists a change in its state and will continue sidedrifting or moving up or down in the trend unless there's a change in sentiment that causes a change in momentum.

The sharemarket is transparent; anyone can access the internet to see orders that have transacted, with price and volume, as well as orders that haven't yet transacted. As I've pointed out in previous chapters, it's usually best to go with an established trend because it's a less risky strategy than going against it. There may be some traders who trade against a trend (contrarians) but they're in the minority, so once a trend develops it tends to gather pace and continue moving in the same direction with continuing momentum. The concept of momentum in the sharemarket applies to individual shares and also to the market as a whole.

Tip

Share prices will remain at rest (sideways drift) or continue moving in the same uptrend or downtrend unless a change in sentiment causes a change in momentum.

Momentum and trends

Let's now see how momentum applies to shares in each of the three main basic trend modes: sidetrend, uptrend and downtrend.

Sidetrend momentum

When the share price is in a sidetrend the price bounces around between support and resistance levels with insufficient force to break free of these constraints. A short increase in momentum drives the price up from the support level but the change is short-lived and runs out of puff when the resistance level is reached. Then there's a change in the other direction, but again it's short-lived and peters out when the support level is reached. This bouncing between levels will continue indefinitely unless there's a significant change in sentiment that causes a substantial change in momentum and pushes the price up beyond the resistance level or down below the support level. As I discussed in chapter 3, traders who identify the support and resistance channel can make short-term profits by buying around the support price and selling around the resistance price.

Uptrend and downtrend momentum

An uptrending or downtrending share price continues moving in the same direction because of its momentum. The initial sentiment change that started the trend can lose relevance and the trend can continue because its own momentum keeps it going! To see how this works, let's consider a share price that's in a sidetrend channel bouncing around between a support level of 90¢ and a resistance level of $1.00. One day the company announces a significant favourable change in fortunes and traders reading the announcement decide to buy. Excess demand drives up the price and it breaches the resistance level. The closing price that day is $1.10. The next day other traders note the price rise above the long-term resistance level and regard this as a major move, so they place purchase orders. That day the price rises again and closes at $1.15.

Now an uptrend is in progress, and on successive trading days more and more traders jump onboard the uptrend. They are not concerned with the initial change that started the trend; they just see a share price going up and they want to get in on the action. The trend gathers pace and continues, with the price rising beyond a 'reasonable' level, which might have been $1.30 as determined by intrinsic value based on realistic earnings expectations. Some time later, traders who bought into the trend in the early stages take profits and the excess of sell orders drives the price down. Now there's a trend reversal and momentum starts to gather pace in the opposite direction. When the price falls to what's considered by some traders to represent good value these traders place buy orders, so the downtrend falters and bounces back up again.

A possible scenario based on the Elliott wave theory (see chapter 4) is that the price at which the downtrend reversal occurs is likely to be 62% of the initial price rise. So if the price rose 50¢ above the initial resistance level of $1.00 to $1.50 before reversing, the theory predicts a fall of 62% of 50¢, or 31¢, to $1.19 before the new downtrend reverses again. This sequence of events is illustrated in figure 7.1.

Figure 7.1: price wave sequence

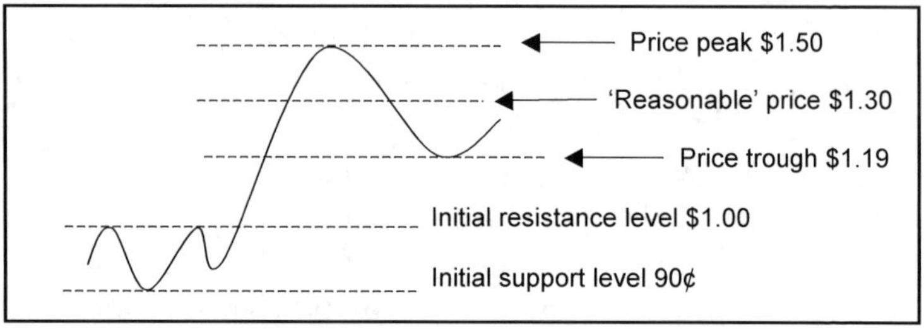

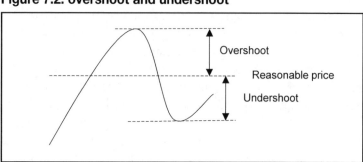

Overshoot and undershoot

Because share prices have momentum, trends can gather pace and prices can rise higher than is reasonably justified in an uptrend or lower in a downtrend. This is known as overshoot and undershoot, and is illustrated in figure 7.2.

Figure 7.2: overshoot and undershoot

Overshoot is also known as overbought and undershoot as over-sold, and are examples of overreaction caused by momentum.

Recognising overbought and oversold levels

There are two different methods you can use to help identify overbought and oversold levels. These are:

⇨ *a fundamental analysis approach:* estimate a reasonable (or realistic) price using fundamental factors. For example, if an uptrend begins as a consequence of the announcement of a more favourable profit result than was previously expected, you can work out a new realistic price using the price to earnings ratio based on the new earnings per share

⇨ *a technical analysis approach:* use a technical analysis indicator to identify overbought or oversold levels.

Because this book is about technical analysis I won't discuss the fundamental analysis method any further, but you can investigate this method in greater detail in *Teach Yourself About Shares* or *Shares Made Simple*. In the technical analysis method there are several indicators that have been developed to identify overbought or oversold levels. In this chapter I'll focus on the momentum indicator, and in later chapters I'll discuss others that have a similar purpose.

Tip

There are two different approaches that you can use to help identify overbought and oversold price levels. These are the fundamental analysis approach and the technical analysis approach. Both are useful approaches and can be used in conjunction with one another.

Momentum indicator

The momentum indicator is based on a very simple calcula-tion. It's just the difference between today's closing price and the closing price a number of days ago. The default number of days is usually about 10 or 12. If you're using a weekly frequency, the momentum calculation will be based on the closing price this week and the closing price 10 or 12 weeks ago. Sometimes the charting software allows you to vary the number but I suggest you stick to the default value.

To illustrate the momentum calculation, consider table 7.1; I've calculated the momentum based on daily frequency. To simplify the table I've used only a five-day time period, and to help clarify the calculation I've repeated the price five days ago in the third column.

Table 7.1: momentum calculation

Day	Closing price ($)	Closing price five days ago ($)	Momentum ($)
1	4.18	–	–
2	4.12	–	–
3	4.14	–	–
4	4.21	–	–
5	4.25	–	–
6	4.28	4.18	0.10
7	4.26	4.12	0.14
8	4.29	4.14	0.15

Like moving averages, which are also based on a retrospective time period, the momentum for the first days of the period (in this case five) can't be calculated. This won't be evident when you look at the momentum indicator on a charting site because the software will automatically go back to earlier data.

The momentum indicator can be positive or negative depending on whether later prices are higher or lower than earlier prices. In table 7.1 you can see that the momentum is positive because the later prices in days 6, 7 and 8 are higher than earlier prices in days 1, 2 and 3.

The momentum indicator is charted as a separate chart below the main price chart and may be shown as a bar chart or line chart. It is best used with relatively short time period charts; it loses significance over longer time periods.

Tip

Use the momentum indicator with daily charts over a period of one year or less.

Momentum trading strategies

In an uptrend when shares become overbought a downward price correction is most likely, and in a downtrend when shares are oversold an upward price correction is most likely. If the price approaches the overbought condition in an uptrend you need to consider selling and taking profits, and when the price bounces back from an irrational low point in an oversold condition it's a good time to consider buying.

The momentum indicator tends to follow the trend and change direction as the trend reverses. The indicator will generally be positive in an uptrend and negative in a down-trend. In a downtrend the indicator moves down into negative territory, and as the trend reverses the indicator also reverses and heads toward the zero line. If the uptrend is sustained, the indicator will cross the zero line and remain in positive territory, but if the uptrend reverses the indicator will reverse and head down again.

Therefore momentum indicator trading signals are:

⇨ buy (go long) if momentum is negative and turns upwards

⇨ sell shares you already hold (or go short) if momentum is positive and turns downwards.

You'll probably recognise that these trading signals are similar to MACD signals indicating trend reversals. Like MACD signals, momentum signals are most effective when momentum changes take place at the more extreme positions and not close to the zero axis. If the momentum indicator bounces around fairly close to the zero axis I suggest you ignore these bounces. As a rule of thumb, take heed of momentum changes only when they occur in the region that's outside 50% of the momentum range. It may be helpful to draw horizontal lines on the momentum chart at the 50% levels above and below the zero momentum line to indicate significant levels. You won't be able to do this precisely because the momentum won't always range to exactly the same high and low positions, but you'll be able to get approximate levels that will be sufficiently accurate for the purpose.

Tip

Momentum changes close to the zero line are generally not significant and should be ignored. Significant momentum levels are 50% or more of the extreme momentum values.

Example 1

Figure 7.3 is an OHLC chart with 13-day and 31-day EMAs taken from the Incredible Charts site showing 12-day momentum for OZ Minerals (OZL) over a 9-month time period. I've expanded the chart a little vertically to make it easier to read. (By now I assume you're sufficiently at home with moving averages that you can differentiate between the 13-day EMA and the 31-day EMA without needing me to mark them.)

On the momentum chart I've inserted two dashed lines at positions about 50% above and below the momentum range.

I've marked momentum trading signals that lie beyond the 50% levels, as follows:

1	buy	6	sell
2	sell	7	sell
3	buy	8	buy
4	sell	9	sell.
5	buy		

Figure 7.3: momentum

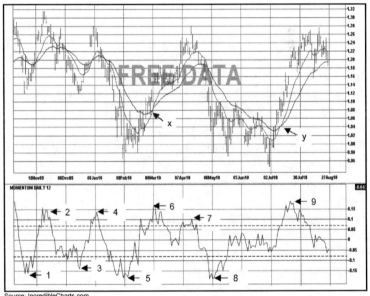

Source: IncredibleCharts.com

You can see that the momentum indicator often signals a trend change before the moving averages cross over. However, there are two significant points of divergence, and in both cases the momentum indicator gives an unreliable signal. Points 'x' and 'y' are moving average golden cross buy signals, whereas the momentum indicator (points 6 and 9) indicates that the price is in the overbought region and as the momentum turns down it gives a contradictory signal to sell.

Advantages and limitations of the momentum indicator

The main advantage of the momentum indicator is that it's very responsive to price changes. This is because it's based on a single price difference only: today's closing price compared to the closing price some days ago. As we've seen, indicators such as moving averages and MACD are calculated by averaging prices over a number of time periods and therefore these indicators are lagging indicators. On the other hand, the momentum indicator responds immediately to price changes without the lag inevitable with an averaging indicator.

However, this very strength of the momentum indicator is also its weakness because there's no smoothing. Momentum often oscillates and gives signals that would result in whipsaw trades if acted on in isolation. Also bear in mind that, like moving averages and MACDs, the momentum indicator is based on a single price each period (closing price) and ignores the price range during the period.

Nevertheless, the momentum indicator is widely used to identify overbought and oversold levels. Because the momentum indicator doesn't always give reliable indications, I suggest you use it only as a filter in conjunction with price trends and primary indicators (such as moving averages and MACDs). If the momentum indicator provides confirmation you can be more confident in your analysis, but if it doesn't then the divergence needs further investigation.

Tip

Use the momentum indicator only as a filter; that is, a secondary tool used in conjunction with other primary tools that are less prone to oscillate and give misleading signals.

Example 2

It's now time to try your hand at reading and marking up a momentum chart. The chart in figure 7.4, from the Incredible Charts site, is a 6-month OHLC chart for Santos (STO) with 13-day and 31-day EMAs shown. Mark the momentum indications and also mark any golden or dead crosses indicated by the moving averages. My interpretation is given in appendix figure A7.4.

Figure 7.4: OHLC chart with momentum

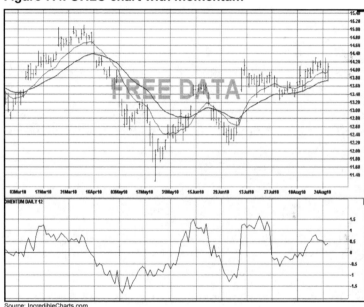

Source: IncredibleCharts.com

Chapter summary

⇨ Momentum in trading markets is a very similar concept to momentum in the physical world. Physical momentum occurs because bodies remain in a state of rest or uniform motion unless some force causes a change in that state. In trading markets, share prices also tend to follow an established trend unless a force causes a change, and that force is a change in trader sentiment triggered by an announcement or a rumour.

⇨ When the share price is drifting sideways it can remain in this state for a long time, until some major change in sentiment causes a break out from the sidetrend channel.

⇨ Shares in an uptrend or downtrend often overshoot or undershoot because momentum drives the price beyond a 'reasonable' level as determined by a rational analysis of the effects of the change that initially caused the change in sentiment.

⇨ Overshoot in an uptrend is known as an overbought condition and undershoot in a downtrend as an oversold condition.

⇨ The momentum indicator helps to identify overbought or oversold conditions. It's simply the difference between today's closing price and the closing price some days ago (usually 10 or 12).

⇨ The momentum indicator is usually shown as a bar chart or line chart below the main price chart.

⇨ The momentum indicator can be positive or negative and will periodically cross above or below zero. It tends to be positive in uptrends and negative in downtrends.

⇨ It's best to use the momentum indicator with charting time periods of six months to one year.

⇨ Momentum indicator trading signals are: buy (go long) if momentum is negative and turns upwards and sell existing holdings (or go short) if momentum is positive and turns downwards.

⇨ Momentum trading signals are similar to MACD signals indicating trend reversals. Like MACD signals, momentum signals are most effective when momentum changes occur at the more extreme positions. As a rule of thumb, momentum indications are significant only when the momentum moves into a region beyond the 50% range.

⇨ The main advantage of the momentum indicator is that it's very responsive to price changes because there's no averaging involved. However, this is also its weakness as it can oscillate and give misleading signals.

⇨ It's best to use the momentum indicator as a filter (in conjunction with other indicators) and not as a primary trading tool.

chapter 8

Relative strength index

In chapter 7 I discussed how momentum operates in trading markets causing overshoot or undershoot; that is, overbuying in an uptrend and overselling in a downtrend. I also described the momentum indicator that's used to track momentum and highlight overbought or oversold conditions. In this chapter I'll describe another widely used indicator that's used for essentially the same purpose: the relative strength index (RSI).

A measure of momentum

The relative strength index was developed in 1978 by Welles Wilder Jr. The name relative strength index is really a misnomer because the index is a measure of momentum; it's not a comparison of the strength of one stock to another stock or index. Like momentum, its purpose is to identify overbought and oversold conditions, but it differs from the momentum indicator in that it's based on a number of values and not a single value. This makes it slower to respond to price changes than the momentum indicator but also makes it a more reliable indicator.

Tip

The RSI indicator tends to be more reliable than the momentum indicator for identifying overbought or oversold levels and giving trading signals.

RSI calculation

The RSI can be calculated in a number of different ways, but the easiest way is as follows:

1   The RSI is based on a time period (or term) that's usually in the range 7 to 21 days, with 14 days being common.

2   Days are classified according to whether they are up days or down days. An up day is when the closing price is higher than the opening price, whereas a down day is a day when the closing price is lower than the opening price.

3   The total of the up-day closing prices and down-day closing prices during the term is calculated.

4   The total of the up-day prices is divided by the total of the up-day and down-day prices.

5   The ratio obtained in step 4 is multiplied by 100 to obtain the RSI (as a percentage).

6   The procedure is repeated with each successive day and a new RSI is calculated.

I described the RSI calculation above using a daily frequency but if you're using a weekly frequency the same principles apply using weeks instead of days.

The shorter the term of the RSI, the quicker it will respond to price trend changes but also the greater it's volatility.

Unlike momentum, the RSI can't be negative but fluctuates between a minimum of 0% and a maximum of 100%. If all days in the RSI term are up days the RSI will be 100%, and if all the days are down days it will be 0%. A neutral day (where the closing price doesn't change) is disregarded.

Some charting software uses a slightly different RSI calculation that's based on the average of the up days and down days in the period. In some cases, the average may not be a simple average but an exponential average that gives more weight to recent prices than earlier ones.

Example 1

I've demonstrated the RSI calculation in table 8.1. For simplicity's sake I've used a seven-day term.

Table 8.1: RSI calculation (seven day)

Day	Opening price ($)	Closing price ($)	U or D	Sum U ($)	Sum D ($)	Sum U + D	RSI (%)
1	1.00	1.02	U	–	–	–	–
2	1.05	1.07	U	–	–	–	–
3	1.06	1.06	–	–	–	–	–
4	1.07	1.05	D	–	–	–	–
5	1.06	1.04	D	–	–	–	–
6	1.05	1.09	U	–	–	–	–
7	1.08	1.10	U	4.28	2.09	6.37	67.2
8	1.11	1.11	–	3.26	2.09	5.35	60.9
9	1.11	1.09	D	2.19	3.18	5.37	40.8
10	1.08	1.10	U	3.29	3.18	6.47	50.9

Note that in this example days 3 and 8 are neutral days and therefore are not considered in the calculation.

Interpreting the RSI

The RSI indicator is charted as a line chart below the price chart. As I've said, the RSI will always be positive and range in value from 0 to 100. The RSI seldom reaches the extreme low of 0 or high of 100 because it's very rare to have a succession of all up days or down days during a 14-day term. (It would be rather like tossing a coin and getting 14 heads in a row.) A high majority of up days during the RSI term indicates an overbought condition with a downward correction most likely, and a high majority of down days indicates an oversold condition with an upward correction most likely.

Overbought and oversold levels

Overbought and oversold RSI levels of 70 and 30 are usually used, but this is not set in concrete and there are different interpretations. Other levels used include 80–20 and 60–40. Some charting software automatically shows overbought and oversold levels with lines on the RSI chart but other software doesn't do this and leaves it for you to define your own overbought and oversold levels.

I've illustrated overbought and oversold regions on an RSI chart in figure 8.1.

Figure 8.1: RSI with overbought and oversold regions

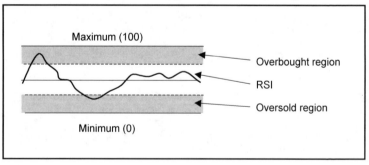

Tip

Use 70–30 RSI levels to identify overbought and oversold regions unless you have a good reason to use other values.

Example 2

Now let's look at a typical RSI chart below a price chart, as shown in figure 8.2.

Figure 8.2: price chart with RSI

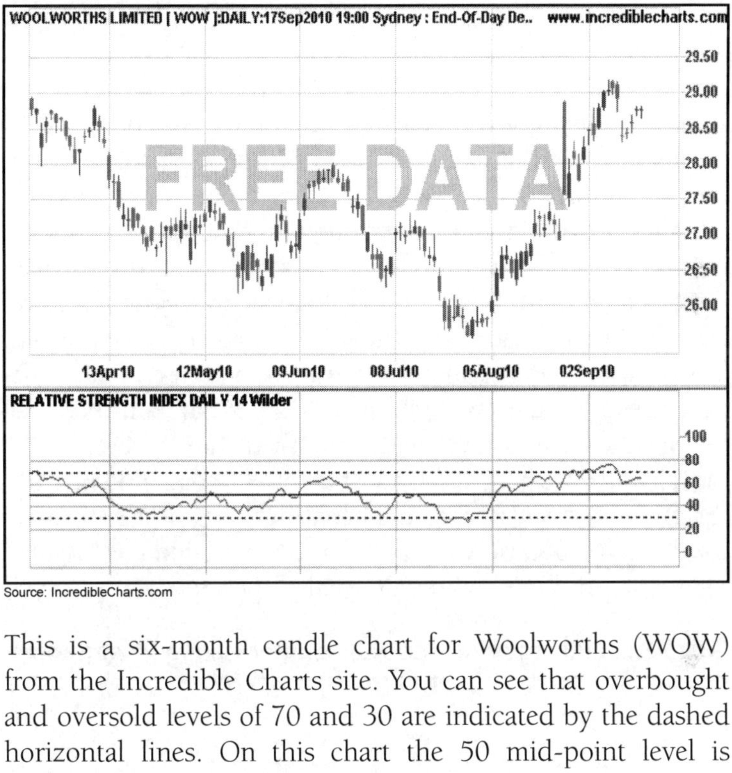

WOOLWORTHS LIMITED [WOW]:DAILY:17Sep2010 19:00 Sydney : End-Of-Day De.. www.incrediblecharts.com

Source: IncredibleCharts.com

This is a six-month candle chart for Woolworths (WOW) from the Incredible Charts site. You can see that overbought and oversold levels of 70 and 30 are indicated by the dashed horizontal lines. On this chart the 50 mid-point level is indicated by a solid horizontal line.

RSI trends

As a general rule the RSI trends in a similar way to the price, and the following relationships between RSI and price will occur:

⇨ In a price uptrend the RSI trends up.

⇨ In a price downtrend the RSI trends down.

⇨ In a price sidetrend the RSI tends to track sideways, fluctuating up and down around the 50% level without reaching the overbought or oversold regions.

⇨ In a price trend reversal the RSI reverses in the same direction as the price trend.

These are general relationships, and exceptions do occur. Like a candle chart, the RSI defines up and down days by comparing opening and closing prices so it's possible to get a succession of RSI up days (closing price higher than opening price) even though the closing price is trending down. In this case a line chart of the price will downtrend but the RSI won't necessarily follow this trend. This is known as a divergence; it's not a common situation but it does occur occasionally. I've illustrated this situation in figure 8.3 with a succession of up days drawn as white candles. After opening (base of bar), the price rises each day to close higher (top of bar), but because the closing price is lower each day than the day before the line chart (drawn through closing prices) will downtrend. The RSI will track in a manner that depends on the relative number of up and down days prior to this period but it won't follow the price trend and will usually uptrend.

Figure 8.3: closing price and RSI counter trends (divergence)

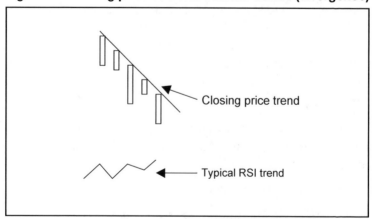

The reverse situation can also occur when a line chart of prices uptrends and the RSI doesn't follow this trend but moves toward a downtrend.

Tip

The RSI generally trends in the same direction as the price but on some occasions the closing price and RSI may counter trend.

Sustained price trend divergence

Another divergence between price and RSI trends occurs in a strong price uptrend or downtrend; that is, one that continues for an extended period. The RSI initially tracks in the direction of the trend, but because it can't exceed the extreme limits of 0 and 100 the RSI tends to flatten out and track sideways as the trend continues. This situation is illustrated in figure 8.4.

Figure 8.4: RSI flattening in continuing uptrends and downtrends

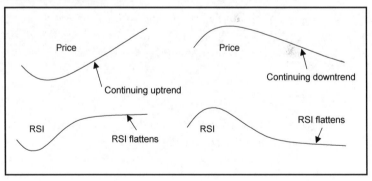

Tip

In sustained price uptrends or downtrends the RSI may track sideways for an extended period.

Trading signals using the RSI

The clearest trading signal appears when the RSI tracks up into the overbought region or tracks down into the oversold region. When the RSI reaches the overbought condition it's generally interpreted as a sell (or avoid) signal, and when the RSI reaches the oversold condition it's a buy signal. However, as I've just pointed out, in sustained uptrends and downtrends the RSI signal won't usually be a good one to act on. If you act immediately on a sell signal you may lose a good deal of the potential profit that's available as the price uptrend continues. Similarly, if you act too quickly on an RSI buy signal you may buy at too high a price as the downtrend continues after the RSI signal first appears.

For these reasons I believe it's better to use the RSI tracking into overbought or oversold levels as a preliminary or cautionary signal, and to use the following RSI signals as more reliable ones for identifying trend turning points:

⇨ *Sell (or short) signal:* the RSI tracks up into the overbought region and then tracks down below it and the price trend also changes direction from up to down.

⇨ *Buy (long) signal:* the RSI tracks down into the oversold region and then tracks up above it and the price trend also changes direction from down to up.

Tip

RSI signals are most reliable when they're considered in conjunction with price trend changes.

Example 3

I'll now revisit figure 8.2 and identify significant RSI indications in figure 8.5.

Figure 8.5: price chart with RSI indications

Source: IncredibleCharts.com

I've numbered the significant indications as follows:

1   Sell signal as the RSI reaches the overbought level and turns down and the price also peaks and turns down. This signal seems unreliable as the price recovers soon after, but is vindicated when the price again turns down with the RSI also turning down.

2   The RSI reaches a low and turns up as the price does the same. This isn't a true buy signal as the RSI doesn't quite reach the oversold level of 30. However, it does indicate an end to the downtrend.

3   The RSI reaches a low and turns up as the price churns but then bounces up. Again this is not a true buy signal as the RSI doesn't quite reach the oversold level of 30. However, it provided quick trading profits for a short-term trader as the price rises steeply afterward.

4   The RSI reaches a high and turns down as the price does the same, but this is not a true sell signal as the RSI doesn't quite reach the overbought level of 70. However, it indicates an end to the short uptrend as the price falls again.

5   The RSI just touches the oversold level before turning up as the price also turns up. This signal isn't a very reliable one as the uptrend isn't sustained.

6   A classic buy signal as the RSI moves up from below the oversold level as the price tracks in the same manner. This proves to be an excellent signal as the price uptrend develops into a sustained one.

7   A classic sell signal as the RSI reaches the overbought level and turns down and the price also peaks and turns down.

If you had bought at point 6 for about $25.50 and sold at point 7 for about $29.00 you'd have made a profit of about $3.50 and that's a return of about 12.8% on the average capital invested of $27.25. As the time period was about six weeks, that's an equivalent annualised return of over 100%.

Even though the RSI didn't quite reach the overbought or oversold levels at points 2, 3 and 4, the price did react in the way indicated by the RSI.

Figure 8.5 shows a dramatic example of a down day where the closing price rose (was higher than the day before). I've marked this as point 8 on the price chart. The RSI didn't reflect this change at all.

Double top or bottom divergences

As well as the trading signals I've outlined, price–RSI divergences at double tops or bottoms can also be used as trading signals. It's an example of the situation that can occur in technical analysis where there's a divergence between a price and indicator trend that provides a useful signal.

The divergence signals are:

⇨ *Uptrend divergence:* the price double tops, reaching the same or a new high, then turns down, but the RSI doesn't double top to a new high.

⇨ *Downtrend divergence:* the price double bottoms, reaching the same or a new low, then turns up, but the RSI doesn't double bottom to a new low.

These price–RSI divergences are illustrated in figure 8.6. For simplicity's sake I've shown the price as a line chart, but when looking at an actual chart it's better to use an OHLC or candle chart.

Figure 8.6: double top and bottom divergences

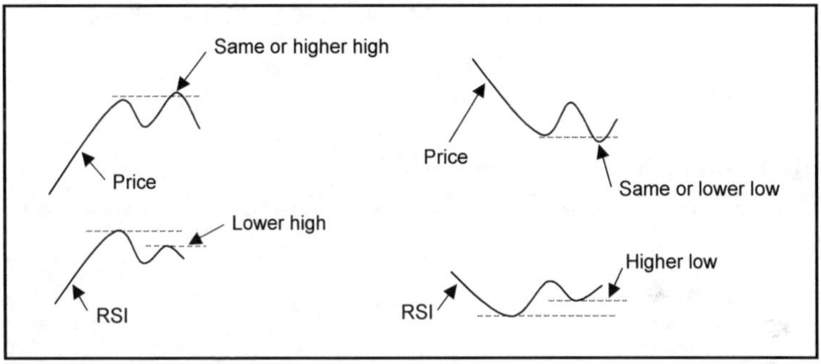

The trading signals are:

⇨ *Sell (or short) signal:* in an uptrend the price double tops to the same or a new high then turns down, but the RSI double tops to a lower high.

⇨ *Buy (long) signal:* in a downtrend the price double bottoms to the same or a new low then turns up, but the RSI double bottoms to a higher low.

Price and RSI double top or bottom divergences are most reliable only when they occur in or close to the overbought or oversold levels and aren't too far apart. A good rule of thumb is that they should occur within about two months.

If you examine figure 8.5 again, you'll notice examples of reliable divergence buy signals at points 2, 3 and 6, where the price double bottoms to a new low but the RSI doesn't follow suit.

Tip

Price and RSI divergences don't occur very often but can provide reliable trading signals, especially when the first RSI peak reaches the overbought level of 70 in an uptrend and when the first RSI trough reaches the oversold level of 30 in a downtrend.

Example 4

Figure 8.7 is a price chart with the RSI indicator shown. It's a six-month candle chart for Tassal Group (TGR) taken from the Incredible Charts site.

Figure 8.7: candle chart with RSI

Source: IncredibleCharts.com

As an exercise, examine this chart and identify significant points and RSI trading signals, including any divergences. I've shown my interpretation in appendix figure A8.7.

Chapter summary

⇨ The RSI indicator (like the momentum indicator) identifies overbought and oversold price levels. Unlike momentum that's based on a single price, the RSI amalgamates a number of prices over the term of the RSI. This makes it less sensitive to trend changes but also makes it a more reliable indicator.

⇨ The term of the RSI can vary from 7 to 21 days, with a default value of 14 days being common. The shorter the term of the RSI, the more sensitive it is to trend changes but the lower the reliability of the indication.

⇨ The RSI distinguishes up days and down days using the criteria that up days occur when the closing price is higher than the opening price and down days when the closing price is lower.

⇨ The RSI is calculated by obtaining the sum (or average) of the up days and dividing it by the sum (or average) of the up days plus the down days. The ratio is converted to a percentage.

⇨ The RSI is always positive and can vary between extreme limits of 0 and 100.

⇨ Traditionally RSI levels of 70 and 30 are used to identify overbought and oversold levels, but these levels can be changed according to personal preferences and risk profiles.

⇨ As a general rule the RSI tends to trend in the same direction as the price.

⇨ The RSI won't follow the trend if the closing price rises in a down day or falls in an up day (or series of them).

⇨ In a prolonged price uptrend or downtrend, after reaching high or low levels the RSI tends to flatten out.

⇨ The simplest trading signals are obtained when the RSI tracks into the overbought region or the oversold region. When the RSI reaches the overbought region this warns that the uptrend may falter, and when the RSI reaches the oversold region this indicates that the downtrend may change.

⇨ The simple RSI trading signals aren't always reliable; more reliable signals occur when the RSI changes direction after reaching the overbought or oversold levels and the price does the same.

⇨ Double top or bottom divergences between the price and the RSI are usually good signals. An uptrend divergence sell signal occurs when the price double tops to the same or a higher high but the RSI doesn't follow suit. A downtrend divergence buy signal occurs when the price double bottoms to the same or a lower low but the RSI doesn't follow suit.

⇨ The RSI shouldn't be used in isolation but in conjunction with price trends and primary trend indicators such as moving averages.

chapter 9

Volume

In this chapter I'll explain the significance of volume in conjunction with price trends. I'll discuss in greater detail the equi-volume chart and outline an important volume indicator known as on balance volume (OBV).

Volume recap

I've mentioned volume in previous chapters so first I'll briefly summarise some important points:

⇨ Volume is the number of transactions in each trading period, so on a daily chart it's the number of trades each day and on a weekly chart the number of trades each week.

⇨ Every trade involves both a buy and a sell transaction, so volume is the number of shares purchased or the number of shares sold as these numbers must be exactly equal.

⇨ Demand is the number of shares ordered (bids) and supply is the number of shares offered (offers). The market price depends on the number of shares bid and the number of shares offered, and when demand exceeds supply the price will rise, whereas when supply exceeds demand the price will fall.

⇨ Volume is shown as a histogram below the price chart with the height of the bars being proportional to the volume. The scale is usually indicated on a y axis at the side of the histogram.

⇨ Volume trends can be identified by joining the tops of the histogram bars. Volume trends aren't as sustained or easily identified as price trends and volume changes can occur in almost random fashion.

⇨ You can look at the volume histogram in conjunction with the price chart to form an impression of the strength of a price trend.

⇨ Another tool you can use to correlate volume and price is the equi-volume chart. However, this chart isn't always available (for example, it's not available with the CommSec charting facility).

Importance of volume

Volume is important because volume defines the strength of a trend. Generally speaking, the lower the volume the less confidence you can have in the trend or trend change. The greater the volume, the higher your confidence that the trend will continue or that the trend change will be sustained and not transitory.

A useful analogy with volume is to regard it as being similar to water flow in a river. When the river is high, the flow is large and powerful and not easily changed or diverted. When the river is low, the flow is weak and easily changed or diverted and could even peter out entirely. So it is with share trade volume in that low-volume trends or changes in trend are weak and are far more likely to peter out than those based on high volume.

Tip

Trends or trend changes on low volume aren't as significant as those on high volume.

Volume spikes

In the volume histogram you'll often see spikes showing sudden and dramatic increases in volume. These may coincide with significant price changes (particularly gaps), but at times you'll see volume spikes without any significant price change and these might cause you to wonder why there was such a sudden flurry of trading activity. Sometimes spikes precede a price change and these spikes suggest that some traders are acting on knowledge that's not known to the general market. Insider trading is of course illegal but it's a practice that's very difficult to control or eliminate entirely.

Tip

Volume spikes (like price gaps) are worth investigating to try to ascertain causes. Even if there's no obvious cause, spikes indicate a sudden increase in trading activity and that's an important clue that something's in the wind.

Volume and liquidity

Volume is a measure of liquidity; that's to say, when there's a high trade volume on all or most trading days the share involved has high liquidity. Illiquid shares trade infrequently, and sometimes there's no transactions at all in a trading day or on several trading days in succession.

Trading shares with high liquidity has the benefit that you can readily buy or sell, and there's usually only a small spread (price difference) between bids and offers.

High market cap stocks (market leaders) are usually liquid; there's lots of action each trading day. Low market cap stocks can have low liquidity and tend to be more volatile. When the majority of shares are held by a relatively small number of shareholders the stock tends to be relatively illiquid.

Tip

Illiquid stocks are more risky to trade because there might't be a matching trader for a transaction. There might't be a buyer at your target price when you want to sell, so you'll have to accept a low price in order to trade. On the other hand, when you want to buy you may have to offer a higher price than you really want to.

Example 1

To demonstrate the importance of volume, consider the following scenario.

Yesterday the shares closed at $1.02. Today they open at $1.02, and 1 million shares trade during the day, and the price rises to $1.04. This exhausts most buyers. Just prior to market close the situation is as shown in table 9.1.

Table 9.1: market depth

Bids			Offers		
No.	Qty	Pr.	Pr.	Qty	No.
2	80 000	$1.00	$1.04	50 000	1

Now a seller comes in with a small parcel of 1000 shares to offload. The seller places a market order and accepts the bid of $1.00 and the trade takes place without any further transactions before market close.

The statistics for that day's trading will show that over a million shares were traded, and it's a down day because the closing price of $1.00 is lower than the opening price of $1.02 and also lower than yesterday's close of $1.02. The vast majority of shares traded with rising prices but one small seller caused a price fall because this seller placed a market order.

You might wonder why this seller was prepared to sell at a 4% discount compared to the next closest seller. The most likely reason is because the 4¢ a share discount on 1000 shares equates to only $40, a relatively trivial amount. On the other hand, for the next closest seller with 50 000 shares the same 4¢ price drop on 50 000 shares equates to $2000. That's a far more significant amount, so this seller's not prepared to sell at market price.

Conclusion

Although this scenario is a hypothetical it's one that can occur, particularly with the more speculative types of shares where there's often a significant spread between the closest bids and offers. It demonstrates why you need to consider volume in conjunction with a price change and how low-volume trades can distort the overall picture. Such situations are rather like an intercept try or breakaway goal that's scored by one side against the general run of play.

Tip

Low-volume trades can give a false impression of price trends and trend changes because fairly large price differences on low volume can amount to far less total dollars than low price differences on high volumes.

Volume and trend strength

As a general rule, the greater the volume the stronger the trend and the lower the likelihood of the trend faltering or changing. The correlation between volume, trend strength and likelihood of a trend change is indicated in table 9.2.

Table 9.2: trend strength, changes and volume

Volume	Trend strength	Trend change
High and/or rising	Strong	Unlikely
Low and/or falling	Weak	Likely

I've illustrated the relationship in figure 9.1 for uptrends and downtrends. I've drawn price and volume trends as straight lines but of course they'll actually be wavy or jagged and there may be volume spikes or price gaps.

Figure 9.1: volume and trend strength for uptrends and downtrends

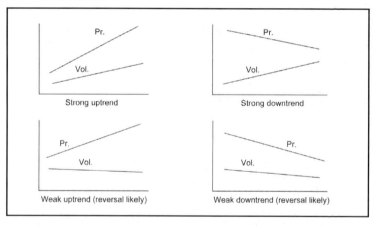

In sidetrend channels the volume is usually fairly steady, but increasing volume can indicate a possible trend breakout. If the price is around the top of the channel the breakout is likely to be upward, whereas if the price is around the bottom of the channel it's likely to be downward. Falling or low volume in a sidetrend usually indicates trader apathy; that's to say, lack of interest in this stock.

Tip

Changes in volume often indicate an imminent trend change.

Smart money and copycat trading

Uptrends or downtrends with increasing volume indicate 'smart money' trading. In an uptrend, astute traders are jumping onboard in the early stages and riding the trend for as long as possible so as to maximise profits. In a downtrend they're selling quickly in the early stages and taking profits before the price falls too much. On the other hand, decreasing volume indicates 'copycat' trading where less astute traders are following the herd. They're getting into an uptrend in the later stages when the trend may be petering out, and in downtrends they're holding on too long and not recognising (or acting on) the downtrend quickly enough.

It's important to recognise trends in the early stages so you can maximise profits in an uptrend and minimise losses in a downtrend. Indeed, you might say that this is the real purpose of chart analysis—to allow you to be a smart trader rather than a copycat.

Tip

High volume in the early stages of a trend indicates 'smart money' trading whereas decreasing volume in the later stages of a trend indicates 'copycat' trading.

Example 2
Figure 9.2 (overleaf) is a typical OHLC chart with volume from the CommSec site.

Figure 9.2: OHLC chart with volume

Source: www.CommSec.com.au

The significant correlations between volume and price are:

⇨ Around position A the volume increases as the price falls to a low. This is a significant turning point, marking the end of the downtrend that changes to an uptrend.

⇨ Between A and B the price drifts essentially sideways and the volume is relatively low.

⇨ At B the volume increases significantly and heralds the commencement of a strong uptrend.

⇨ At C there's a volume spike, but then the volume declines while the uptrend continues. This is a bearish signal indicating that the uptrend is weakening.

There are some other volume spikes that I haven't marked; some coincide with significant trend changes while some don't match any significant features on the price chart. This emphasises the point that volume spikes or changes don't always have a logical connection with price action.

Market depth screen

Before you place any orders it's a good idea to closely examine the market depth screen. This screen summarises the price and volume action for the day to the present time and also the current buy and sell orders (bids and offers) at market. While this screen doesn't indicate trends or trend changes, it does allow you to assess today's action. Importantly, if you're contemplating a trade you can look at the number of shares bid and offered and predict the most likely price move.

Clearly, if there are more shares bid than offered (at prices around the last sale price), the price is likely to rise, and if there are more offered than bid the price is likely to fall.

Tip

If you'd like a detailed explanation of the market depth screen and how to place orders using it please refer to Online Investing on the Australian Sharemarket *or* Teach Yourself About Shares.

Example 3

A typical market depth screen is shown in figure 9.3 (overleaf). It's from the CommSec site and is for the aluminium producer Alumina (AWC).

Looking at this screen you can infer that the price is most likely to fall from the last sale price because there are many more shares on offer (supply) than are bid (demanded) at prices close to the last sale price.

To show this pictorially I've charted demand and supply using Excel, as shown in figure 9.4 (overleaf).

You can clearly see the excess of supply (offers) over demand (bids). This chart is useful, but unfortunately I know of no charting software that provides such a chart.

Figure 9.3: market depth screen

Share Quote as at 2:08 PM Sydney Time, Tuesday, 14 September 2010

◄ ALUMINA LIMITED FPO ► CommSec Margin Lending LVR: 65%

Code	Bid	Offer	Last	Change*	% Change*	Open	High	Low	Volume	Trades	Value	News
AWC	1.870	1.875	1.870	0.000	0.000	1.870	1.885	1.850	8,228,423	1,539	15,385,705	

Buy | Sell | Add to Watchlist | Research | Chart | Course of Sales

Trading Status: **Normal**

Market Depth

	BUY				SELL			52 Week	
Number	Quantity	Price	#	Price	Quantity	Number	High	Low	
14	54,523	1.870	1	1.875	150,081	21	2.060	1.450	
13	111,026	1.865	2	1.880	615,506	26	**Last traded time**		
17	241,458	1.860	3	1.885	404,127	19	14:06:55		
14	230,536	1.855	4	1.890	521,774	30			
22	166,530	1.850	5	1.895	298,342	26			
12	135,762	1.845	6	1.900	1,029,079	61			
12	96,340	1.840	7	1.905	59,515	10			
4	33,629	1.835	8	1.910	379,895	9			
8	159,700	1.830	9	1.915	36,500	5			
4	7,500	1.825	10	1.920	48,025	8			
	321 buyers for 3,464,371 units				390 sellers for 4,800,457 units				

Source: www.CommSec.com.au

Figure 9.4: demand–supply chart

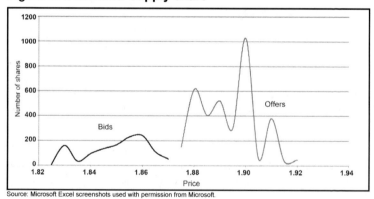

Source: Microsoft Excel screenshots used with permission from Microsoft.

Tip

It's instructive to draw a demand–supply chart using the market depth screen when you're contemplating a trade as it provides a good visual impact of the current demand–supply relationship.

Equi-volume charts

I introduced the equi-volume chart in chapter 2 but now I'll look at it in more detail. This chart is rather similar to a candle chart except that the width of the bars is proportional to the volume and consequently this chart doesn't have a linear x-axis time scale. I'll summarise the important indications on this chart:

⇨ Thin bars indicate low volume and less significance to the price move.

⇨ Long, thin bars (either up or down) indicate large price jumps on small volume.

⇨ Wide bars indicate high volume and more significance to the price move.

⇨ A wide bar on an up day during a downtrend is often a precursor to a trend change to uptrend.

⇨ A wide bar on a down day during an uptrend flashes a warning that the trend may be faltering.

⇨ Squat bars show high volume with a small price change and often mark significant trend change turning points.

Example 4

Figure 9.5 (overleaf) is an equi-volume chart (from Incredible Charts) for Mount Gibson Iron (MGX) over a six-month period. On the website colours (blue and red) are used to denote up days and down days, but in the black and white version in this book the up days appear darker than the down days.

The chart exhibits some interesting features, including classic wave patterns and gaps. At the start of the chart on the left-hand side there's an uptrend with the price peaking at around $2.08 before the trend reverses in early April. The downtrend gathers pace for about a month or so, with the price dropping to below $1.20. Then there's another trend reversal, and the uptrend continues for another month or so with the price reaching about $1.75 before another reversal with the price falling back to $1.40 or so, before reversing again. Toward the end of the chart, a sidetrend establishes with the price hovering around $1.75.

Figure 9.5: equi-volume chart

Source: IncredibleCharts.com

The widest bar on the chart is on an up day that I've marked 'A', which occurs at the bottom of the downtrend. This is a powerful trend reversal signal and an astute trader acting on this signal would have made excellent profits in a short period.

Tip

The equi-volume chart shows price and volume changes in each trading period and makes the relationship between price and volume action easy to interpret. Wide bars often mark trend turning points, particularly if they occur with significant price changes; that's to say, they're long as well as wide.

On balance volume

As we've seen, a problem with an ordinary volume bar chart is that volume trends are difficult to identify because there's no smoothing and volume is usually volatile with many short-term rises, falls and peaks. Fortunately there's an indicator that relates price and volume changes and produces a less volatile curve, and this makes volume trends easier to detect. It was developed in 1963 by Joe Granville and it's known as on balance volume (OBV). Like most other indicators, OBV is shown as a separate chart below the price chart, but unlike volume OBV is charted as a line chart rather than a bar chart (histogram).

An OBV chart has the following features:

⇨ It shows the total (or cumulative) trade volume and not the daily volume.

⇨ If today's closing price is greater than yesterday's closing price, today's volume is added to the OBV total.

⇨ If today's closing price is lower than yesterday's closing price, today's volume is subtracted from the OBV total.

⇨ If today's close is the same as yesterday's close, there's no adjustment to the OBV (regardless of the volume).

The most common frequency used for OBV is daily, but if you're using a weekly frequency with longer term charts the OBV will be based on weekly volumes.

Assuming a daily frequency, the calculation of the OBV is summarised in table 9.3 (overleaf).

It's important to recognise that the distinction between up days and down days is different for OBV compared with the equi-volume chart, candle chart or RSI. In these charts, an up day occurs when the closing price is higher than the opening price for *that day*. In the OBV calculation, an up day occurs when today's closing price is higher than *yesterday's* closing price.

Table 9.3: OBV changes

Today's closing price compared with yesterday's	OBV change
Higher (up day)	Today's volume is added to the OBV total
Lower (down day)	Today's volume is subtracted from the OBV total
Same (no change)	No adjustment to the OBV total

It's also important to realise that OBV reflects the trend in price not just the trend in volume. For example, if the price is rising but the volume is falling, OBV will still rise because on an up day volume is added to the OBV total. So you'll find that OBV tends to mirror the price trend far more than the volume histogram does because the histogram shows volume only without consideration of any price change.

Tip

OBV reflects price trends and not just volume trends.

Example 5

An example of an OBV chart is shown in figure 9.6. It's for the same company as in example 4 (MGX) over the same time period and is from the Incredible Charts site.

In this chart you can clearly see how OBV tends to mirror the price trend. You can also see that the low pivot point in the price chart is matched by a low pivot point in the OBV chart, giving a reinforcement of the trend change signal.

Tip

If a pivot point on a price chart is matched by a pivot point on an OBV chart this reinforces the trend change.

Figure 9.6: OHLC chart with OBV

Source: IncredibleCharts.com

Price–OBV divergence

Price and OBV divergence is indicated when the price double tops to the same (or a higher) high or double bottoms to the same (or a lower) low but the OBV doesn't follow suit. This divergence flashes a warning that there's insufficient volume to sustain the new high or low price. You'll probably recognise that price–OBV divergence is very similar to price–RSI divergence discussed in chapter 8.

I've illustrated price–OBV divergence in figure 9.7 (overleaf). For simplicity's sake, I've shown price as a line chart.

Tip

Price–OBV divergences often indicate that the new price high or low could be unsustainable.

Figure 9.7: price–OBV divergences in uptrends and downtrends

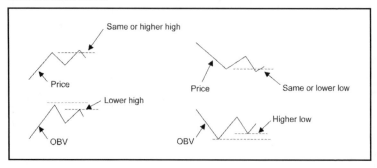

Divergence trading signals

The uptrend divergence indicates that the new price high is most likely unsustainable and the downtrend divergence indicates that the new low is also likely to be unsustainable. These divergences can be used to generate trading signals as follows:

⇨ *Sell (or short) signal:* the price reaches a higher high then turns down while the OBV reaches a lower high and then turns down. This is shown on the left-hand side in figure 9.7.

⇨ *Buy (long) signal:* the price reaches a lower low then turns up while the OBV reaches a higher low and then turns up. This is shown on the right-hand side in figure 9.7.

Tip

Price–OBV divergences can provide useful trading signals.

Reliability of volume indications

Volume trends and volume indicators don't always provide reliable signals. For example, a strong price trend may continue for some time even when the volume is steady or falling. Volume peaks that aren't matched by significant price changes frequently occur and there seems no logical reason for them. Therefore I suggest you don't act on volume changes and volume indicators without taking into account other indicators (such as moving averages, MACD and so on).

Tip

Use volume indications as a filter and not as a primary tool. Volume indications can provide useful additional information but shouldn't be acted on in isolation.

Chapter summary

⇨ It's important to consider volume trends in conjunction with price trends because price trends with thin volume are far less significant than those with high volume.

⇨ Low-volume trades often occur at a significant discount or premium to the last market price because the dollar amounts involved are small. These can distort the general picture indicated by the high-volume trades.

⇨ Volume usually fluctuates considerably from day to day and this volatility makes it difficult to detect volume trends.

⇨ Volume is an indication of trader interest and low volume indicates lethargy; that's to say, traders are disenchanted with the shares and see little reason to buy or sell them.

⇨ Volume spikes indicate sudden change in interest and can be significant when they're accompanied by matching changes in price.

⇨ High or increasing volume usually indicates a strong trend, whereas low or decreasing volume usually indicates a weak trend.

⇨ Increasing volume in the early stages of a trend indicates 'smart money' trading whereas decreasing volume after the trend is established indicates 'copycat' trading. You'll maximise trading profits if you're a smart money trader rather than a copycat.

⇨ The equi-volume chart provides visual correlation between price and volume action. Wide bars often mark trend turning points and are particularly significant when they're accompanied by a significant price change.

⇨ On balance volume is another indicator that allows you to correlate volume action with price action.

⇨ OBV is a total volume and is calculated by adding volume to the total on an up day (closing price higher than the previous close) and subtracting volume from the total on a down day (closing price lower than previous close). No adjustment is made to the total if there's no change in closing price.

⇨ OBV is charted as a line chart below the price chart, and more closely reflects price action than an ordinary volume chart that takes no account of price action.

⇨ When there's a divergence between OBV and price it's often a reliable trading signal. It occurs when the price hits a new high or low but the OBV doesn't follow suit. These divergences indicate that the new price high or low is likely to be unsustainable.

⇨ Volume indications aren't always reliable or logical so it's best to use volume indications as a filter in conjunction with other primary tools.

chapter 10

Bollinger bands

In this chapter I'll discuss Bollinger bands, so named after their inventor John Bollinger. They're another important charting tool that helps you identify trend changes and overbought and oversold conditions, but in a very different way to any other indicator I've outlined.

Bollinger bands are based on the normal distribution so I'll discuss this first.

Normal distribution

In many circumstances we're aware of differences in characteristics; for example, that each human being is a unique person. For some things there are no obvious differences and we assume equality; for example, each bottle of the same product on a supermarket shelf may appear exactly the same to us. In reality they're not—the differences between them may be small but they exist and can be detected with sufficiently accurate measuring equipment.

If you obtain measurements of a particular feature in a population (such as human height or the weight of product in a jar) there'll be some type of distribution to the variation. In the absence of any biasing factors, the variation is most often a symmetrical bell-shaped curve that's known as the normal distribution (for obvious reasons). The normal distribution has a shape as shown in figure 10.1.

Figure 10.1: normal distribution

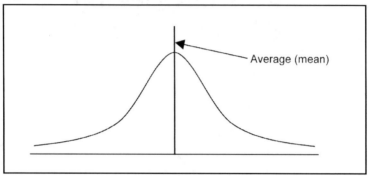

Most data clusters around a central value that's known as the mean or average. It's calculated by adding all the values together and dividing by the number of them. You can get a visual impression of the mean if you imagine the distribution as a cardboard cut out. The mean is located at the horizontal balance position along the x axis. The theoretical (or ideal) normal distribution is symmetrical about the x axis and then the mean will be located at the centre (as shown in figure 10.1).

Spread

The average is an important statistic but it doesn't give any indication of the spread. The spread is the extent of the variation in values above or below the average. Consider figure 10.2.

You can see that both populations cluster about the same average but that population B is spread out more than population A.

A simple measure of spread is the range, which is the largest minus the smallest value, but this isn't a very good indication because it's based on only one extreme high and low value. The best and most statistically accurate measure of spread is known as the standard deviation. I won't describe the mathematical formulation as it's a bit involved and not really relevant to us, but many calculators and spreadsheets have the function built in. Suffice to say that population A would have a lower standard deviation than population B.

Figure 10.2: different spreads

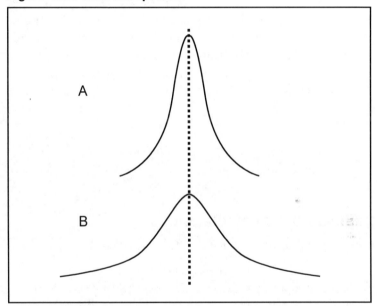

What's of more relevance to us is the mathematical statistic that 95% of the population lies within ± 2 standard deviations and almost all the population (99.7%) lies within ± 3 standard deviations. For example, if the average male height in a population is 190 cm and the standard deviation is 5 cm, then 95% of males will have a height between 180 cm and 200 cm and 99.7% will have a height between

175 cm and 205 cm, because two standard deviations equals 10 cm and three standard deviations equals 15 cm.

Normal distribution applied to charting

You might wonder about the relevance of the normal distribution to share prices and charting. Some chartists argue there's no relevance because share prices are determined by human sentiments which don't conform to any mathematical laws. While this is true, at the same time it's been found that many human traits, including intelligence and personality characteristics, vary in a way that's consistent with the normal distribution. Share prices rise and fall within a certain range and it's possible to calculate an average and standard deviation of the spread in values. As prices change, new values can be calculated; this is the basic principle underpinning Bollinger bands.

Tip

Share prices generally range within limits that can be mathematically calculated.

Bollinger band calculation

Bollinger bands are calculated in the following way:

⇨ An SMA of closing prices is calculated for a number of past time periods. By default, most charting software uses a 20-day SMA.

⇨ The standard deviation of these prices is calculated.

⇨ Prices limits ± 2 standard deviations from the average are calculated.

⇨ At the end of each trading day the average and standard deviation are recalculated, and this process is continued on a moving basis.

If you're charting prices over a fairly long time period and using a weekly frequency the Bollinger bands will be based on weekly closing prices. I seldom use this format and prefer to use the bands with daily frequencies over relatively short time periods (less than one year).

Tip

It's best to use daily frequencies and relatively short time period charts with Bollinger bands.

Charting Bollinger bands

Bollinger bands are drawn on a price chart, which can be a line chart, OHLC chart or candle chart. There are three bands, as follows:

⇨ the mid-band is the average (closing price)

⇨ the upper band is two standard deviations above the average

⇨ the lower band is two standard deviations below the average.

The mid-band line moves up and down but always lies exactly half way between the upper and lower band.

Tip

Even though Bollinger bands are based on closing prices it's best to use an OHLC or candle chart as this enables you to see the daily price range relative to the bands.

Bollinger band interpretation

The mid-band is a 20-day SMA of closing prices and is therefore a smoothed price trendline. However, because it's a moving average it lags the price; that's to say, a trend or trend change indicated by price action won't reflect in the mid-band until 10 days or so later (mid-point of the 20-day period).

The upper and lower bands indicate the range of prices about which the great majority (95%) of prices will fall. Some price bars may overlap an upper or lower band on occasion but it's unusual to find price bars that lie wholly outside the upper or lower bands.

Tip

Interpret the mid Bollinger band as a 20-day SMA smoothed closing price trendline.

Example 1

So much for the theory, let's now look at a chart with Bollinger bands. Figure 10.3 is an OHLC chart from the Incredible Charts site of the All Ordinaries index (XAO) over a nine-month period with Bollinger bands.

Figure 10.3: XAO with Bollinger bands

Source: IncredibleCharts.com

You can see how the bars range above and below the mid-band and sometimes touch the upper or lower band, but in this chart no bar or part of a bar lies outside the upper or lower band.

Note that on the Incredible Charts site the index scale is shown as if it were a price in dollars. To convert this to the equivalent index value, multiply by 100. For example, the value of 50.00 on this chart is an index value of 5000.

Using Bollinger bands as a trading tool

As I've said, some chartists disregard Bollinger bands, but I've found them to be a very useful charting tool. In my opinion Bollinger bands give reliable indications and seldom give misleading signals. They're most useful when used with relatively short term charts (time periods of no more than one year).

An outstanding advantage of Bollinger bands is that unlike many other indicators they're shown on the price chart and not as a separate chart below the price chart. This makes them clear and easy to read, and you can easily relate them to price action. This also means that you have space below the price chart for another indicator without loss of clarity.

A disadvantage of Bollinger bands is that interpretation becomes more difficult when they're shown on a price chart with several moving averages because the moving averages and the mid-band often mingle. On your computer screen different colours will be used but it may still be difficult to clearly distinguish the various lines.

One solution to this problem is to use two different charts: a price chart with moving averages and no Bollinger bands and also a price chart with Bollinger bands and no moving averages. Another option is to call up only one moving average because, as I've said, the mid-band is actually a 20-day SMA. If you're using a relatively short period chart, you could call up a shorter term moving average (in the range 5 to 10 days) if you decide to use this option.

Tip

When using Bollinger bands you'll get the clearest visual impression if you use the OHLC or candle chart format without moving averages. If you want a moving average to be shown, I suggest you call up a relatively short term one.

Bollinger bands and volatility

Volatility is essentially the same as spread; that's to say, the greater the volatility, the greater the range of values that occurs in a relatively short time period. It follows that the width of the Bollinger bands is an indication of volatility, with wide bands indicating high volatility and close bands low volatility.

Example 2

If you look at figure 10.3 again you can see that in February the bands were wide apart, then contracted during March and April before expanding again in May and then remaining approximately constant for the rest of the time.

I've illustrated some band width changes in figure 10.4; these indicate the change in the volatility of the XAO index during the charting period.

Figure 10.4: XAO band separation changes

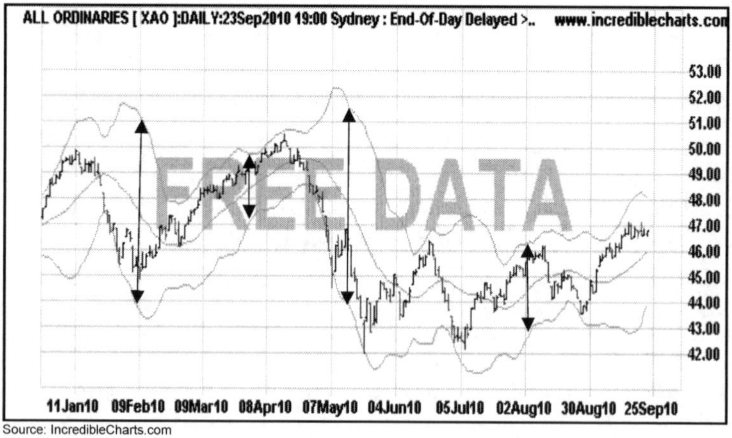

Source: IncredibleCharts.com

Share price volatility

Share price volatility as indicated by Bollinger bands is not the volatility of prices during any one trading session; that's to say, whether there was a large or small difference between high and low prices. Instead, Bollinger band width is an indication of the volatility of closing prices during the period of time for which the Bollinger bands are calculated. So for a 20-day period, large band width indicates that closing prices fluctuated considerably over the last 20 days and small band width indicates that closing prices didn't fluctuate greatly during this period.

High price volatility can have two causes:

⇨ a sustained uptrend or downtrend

⇨ large price changes with one or more significant price gaps.

Low volatility indicates little price range during the period. This is typical in a relatively narrow sidetrend channel. These narrow channels indicate price consensus between buyers and sellers and provide little opportunity for profits, other than for very short term traders.

Tip

The width of Bollinger bands provides a visual impression of closing price volatility. Wide bands indicate a significant uptrend or downtrend or price gapping. Narrow bands usually appear in a sidetrend with prices ranging between fairly close support and resistance levels.

Trends and trend change indications

If you look closely at figure 10.3 (on page 192) you can conclude that trends and trend changes are indicated by the Bollinger bands as follows:

⇨ *Strong uptrend:* the bands are wide apart and incline upward with the top of the bars close to, or touching, the upper band.

⇨ *Strong downtrend:* the bands are wide apart and incline downward with the bottom of the bars close to, or touching, the lower band.

⇨ *Trend change from uptrend to downtrend:* the bars change direction and move away from the upper band, cross the mid-band and move toward to the lower band. The mid-band also changes direction from uptrend to downtrend but lags the bar change.

⇨ *Trend changes from downtrend to uptrend:* the bars change direction and move away from the lower band, cross the mid-band and move toward the upper band. The mid-band also changes direction from downtrend to uptrend but lags the bar change.

⇨ *Sidetrend:* the bands are relatively close together and approximately horizontal. If the sidetrend changes to an uptrend or downtrend the mid-band will trend in the same direction as the bars but the band change will lag the bar change.

As I've said, when a trend change occurs the mid-band changes direction but lags the change because it's based on a 20-day moving average that doesn't immediately reflect a trend change. The upper and lower bands don't always change direction together; often the upper band is rising while the lower band is falling and vice versa. This comes about because the trend change increases the band width (volatility); the bands move further apart. The mid-band gives a more reliable indication of the trend change than the upper or lower bands as it's a 20-day moving average and it doesn't reflect volatility.

Tip

It's best to look at the mid-band for confirmation of a trend change as this band gives a more reliable indication than the upper or lower band, but bear in mind that the mid-band lags the change by 10 days or so.

Example 3

To illustrate Bollinger band time lags, I'll now revisit figure 10.3 and mark the significant time lags between the index trend change and the change in direction of the mid-band.

You can clearly see in figure 10.5 how the mid-band reflects the index trend change but lags it by about 10 days. You can also see that the upper and lower bands don't give a clear indication of the trend change; one band can be rising while the other is falling and vice versa.

Figure 10.5: Bollinger band trend change time lags

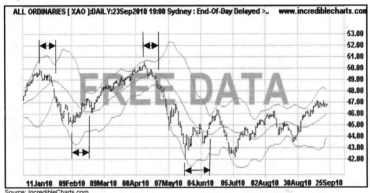

Source: IncredibleCharts.com

Example 4

To illustrate the trend and trend change indications I've outlined, I'll revisit figure 10.3 and mark the significant features as shown in figure 10.6 (overleaf).

I've numbered points as follows:

1   Uptrend ends and the index reverses direction and moves down from the upper band, crossing the mid-band and down to touch the lower band at point 2.

2   Downtrend ends and the index reverses direction and moves up to cross the mid-band and then moves between the mid-band and the top band in a strong uptrend to point 3.

3   Uptrend ends and the index reverses direction, moving down to cross the mid-band, and clusters around the lower band to point 4.

4   The index moves briefly away from the lower band but doesn't cross the mid-band; it reverses direction and heads down again.

5   The index touches the lower band but this time it reverses direction and continues heading up to cross the mid-band and almost reaches the upper band at point 6.

6   The index reverses direction again and downtrends across the mid-band to touch the lower band at point 7.

7   The index reverses direction again and moves up to cross the mid-band in a new uptrend.

8   The index uptrend reverses to downtrend as the index moves down to touch the lower band at point 9.

9   The index downtrend reverses to uptrend and moves up away from the lower band.

Figure 10.6: Bollinger bands and trend changes

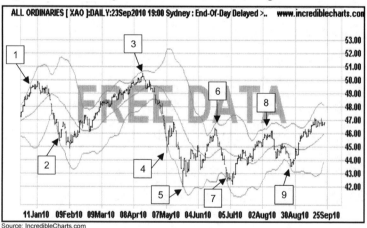

Source: IncredibleCharts.com

Tip

Bollinger bands indicate a trend change when prices clustering around the upper or lower band change direction and move away from the band toward the mid-band.

Bollinger bands and overbought/oversold conditions

On a price chart almost all price bars will lie between the upper and lower bands and often range from one band to another with a wave-like motion. So you might infer that the lower band is equivalent to a moving support level and the upper band is equivalent to a moving resistance level. When prices cluster around the upper band this indicates an overbought condition and that a downward correction is likely. Similarly when prices cluster around the lower band this indicates an oversold condition and that an upward correction is likely.

However, these interpretations are a little too simplistic, and, as we've seen in figure 10.3, in a sustained uptrend or downtrend bars can cluster close to the upper or lower band for a considerable period. Therefore in a sustained uptrend or downtrend you can't reliably use the bands to indicate overbought or oversold levels.

However, in a sidetrend Bollinger bands can provide useful indications of overbought or oversold levels. In chapter 3 I discussed how you can draw horizontal straight lines in a sidetrend to indicate support and resistance levels. With Bollinger bands it's essentially the same idea using the lower and upper bands as support and resistance levels. The difference is that these levels will fluctuate up and down rather than being horizontal.

Tip

In a sidetrend, upper and lower Bollinger bands can be regarded as fluctuating resistance and support levels.

Example 5

I'll now look at a share price chart with Bollinger bands. Figure 10.7 is an OHLC chart for Bluescope Steel (BSL) over an eight-month period taken from the Incredible Charts site.

I've numbered the significant indications as follows:

1   Downtrend completion as the price bars change direction and move away from the lower band.

2   Uptrend commences as the price bars head up and move up away from the lower band.

3   Uptrend reversal as the price bars head down again moving away from the upper band.

4   Downtrend reversal as the price bars change direction and move up away from the lower band. However, this turns out to be an unreliable signal as the downtrend quickly re-establishes until point 5 is reached.

5   Downtrend reversal with the price bars changing direction and moving up away from the lower band. You'll note that one price bar overlaps the lower band here.

6–10   The price moves in waves in essentially a sidetrend pattern, touching the lower band and moving up away from it at points 7 and 9, and touching the upper band and moving down away from it at points 6, 8 and 10. At point 8 one price bar slightly overlaps the upper band.

Figure 10.7: OHLC chart with Bollinger bands

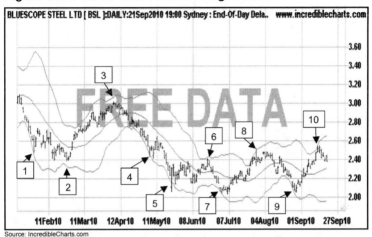

Source: IncredibleCharts.com

Note that many indications in this chart are very similar to those I outlined for the All Ords index in example 4.

Bollinger band trading signals

You can see from example 5 that the Bollinger bands can provide useful trading signals that can lead to profitable short-term trades. Buying soon after point 2 at a price of around $2.50 and selling soon after point 3 at a price of around $2.90 produces a profit of 16% (excluding brokerage) in a time period of about six weeks, and that equates to an annualised return of about 138%. From point 5 to point 10 there are three short-term trading opportunities. The first, from point 5 to 6, isn't very profitable and is about a break even situation because the buy price and sell price are both about $2.30. However, the next two waves from points 7 to 8 and 9 to 10 are very profitable ones. Buying soon after point 7 at about $2.10 and selling soon after point 8 for about $2.40 results in about a 14% profit, and buying in again at point 9 at about $2.10 and selling soon after point 10 for about $2.50 produces a 19% profit. These profits occur in a period of about six weeks each and so equate to excellent annualised returns of over 100% on capital invested.

Tip

Using Bollinger band trading signals can result in profitable short-term trades in all types of trends

Overlapping bars

When bars overlap the upper or lower bands some chartists regard this as a significant trading signal. If only a few bars are involved, I regard this signal as insufficiently reliable to be worth acting on. My reasoning is that Bollinger bands are based on ± 2 standard deviations, which accounts for 95% of the population. Therefore 5% of the population can be expected to lie outside the upper or lower bands, and when a few values lie outside a band it's a normal event and isn't an indication of any significant factors operating.

Tip

If a few bars overlap an upper or lower band don't regard this as a trading signal unless the bars start to change direction and move away from the band.

Example 6

It's now time for you to look at a price chart with Bollinger bands and draw your own conclusions. In figure 10.8 I've reproduced an OHLC chart taken from the Incredible Charts site for Australian Pharmaceutical Industries (API) over a six-month period.

Try to identify the trends, trend changes and volatility. I've given my interpretation in appendix figure A10.8.

Figure 10.8: OHLC chart with Bollinger bands

Source: IncredibleCharts.com

Chapter summary

⇨ Bollinger bands are based on the normal distribution, which occurs frequently with variable data of all types and appears as a symmetrical bell-shaped curve when charted.

⇨ An average value or mean is at the centre of the distribution and the standard deviation is a measure of spread on either side of the mean.

⇨ Bollinger bands have a mid-band that's an SMA calculated on closing prices over the last 20 periods.

⇨ Upper and lower Bollinger bands are spaced at ± 2 standard deviations from the mean.

⇨ An outstanding advantage of Bollinger bands is that they're shown on a price chart and not as a separate chart below the price chart. This makes it easy to relate price action to the bands without loss of clarity.

⇨ When looking at Bollinger bands it's best to use the OHLC or candle chart format with daily frequency and relatively short time periods (less than one year).

⇨ The width of the bands is a reflection of volatility. The further apart the bands are the greater the volatility and the closer together they are the lower the volatility.

⇨ Wide bands on a price chart indicate significant closing price changes in the last 20 periods. These changes can be due to a sustained trend or to one or more significant price gaps. Examination of the price chart will soon reveal the cause.

⇨ In a sustained uptrend price bars move upward, congregating around the upper band, and in a sustained downtrend price bars move downward, congregating around the lower band.

⇨ In a sustained sidetrend price bars range up and down in a wave pattern, touching upper and lower bands that are approximately horizontal.

⇨ In a trend change the price bars move away from the closest band and head toward the mid-band, eventually crossing it and moving toward the other band. The mid-band will also change direction but lags the trend change.

⇨ In a sidetrend, the lower band is equivalent to a fluctuating support level, and prices clustering around this band indicate an oversold condition with upward correction likely. Similarly the upper band is equivalent to a fluctuating resistance level, and prices clustering around this band indicate an overbought condition with downward correction likely.

⇨ As well as providing good longer term trading signals, Bollinger band trading can result in profitable short-term trades in all types of markets.

chapter 11

Money flow

In this chapter I'll discuss several charting indicators that combine price and volume in a different way to the other indicators I've discussed in previous chapters. The money flow indicators I'll discuss are: the money flow index, Chaikin money flow and Twiggs money flow. These indicators are similar in some ways to the momentum indicator, relative strength index (RSI) and on balance volume (OBV), except that they combine price changes and volume changes into one indicator.

Before I discuss them I'll first briefly recap momentum, RSI and OBV:

⇨ *Momentum indicator.* The momentum indicator attempts to indicate overbought/oversold levels (overshoot and undershoot) by calculating the difference between today's closing price and the closing price a number of days ago (usually 10 or 12). It's a very simple indicator that's based purely upon two closing prices. It gives the difference between the two prices in dollar terms (not as a ratio or a percentage) and can be positive or negative.

⇨ *Relative strength index.* The RSI also attempts to indicate overbought/oversold levels. It's not based on only two prices, rather it's based on the total of the closing prices over a number of days (14 is common). If the closing price is higher than the opening price this is an up day, whereas a lower closing price is a down day. The ratio between the sum of all the up-day closes and the sum of all closing prices in the period is converted to a percentage, and that's the RSI. The RSI can't be negative, and ranges from zero (no up days in the period) to 100 (all up days).

⇨ *On balance volume.* On balance volume attempts to indicate the strength of a trend by the volume change accompanying a trend. It's calculated by adding today's volume to the indicator on an up day and subtracting it on a down day. However, the distinction between up days and down days is different to the RSI; when calculating the OBV, today is an up day if today's close is higher than yesterday's close. OBV is a volume total, it's not a percentage and it's always positive.

You can see that these three indicators are calculated using closing prices only or volumes only. Now I'll discuss indicators that combine price and volume. The first indicator I'll discuss is the money flow index, but first we'll look at what money flow is.

As I've previously stated, volume is important because a price move on high volume is more significant than the same move on low volume. The higher the volume, the greater the money flow associated with a price move. The amount of money involved (money flow, or MF) is obtained by multiplying the price by the volume:

$$MF = Price \times Volume$$

You can see that the money flow combines both price and volume in one statistic, and that the same price move will have a high money flow if it's accompanied by high volume rather than low.

The money flow index

Like the RSI, the money flow index (MFI) is conventionally based on a 14-period time frame. Most commonly a daily frequency is used, but if you're using a weekly frequency price chart the index would be based on a 14-week period.

Assuming a 14-day period, the MFI can be calculated in the following way:

⇨ For each day, the average of the closing, high and low price is calculated. For example, if today's closing price is $1.23, with a high of $1.25 and a low of $1.21, then today's average price is: $(1.23 + 1.25 + 1.21) \div 3 = \$1.23$.

⇨ For each day, the money flow is calculated by multiplying the average price by the volume of trades. If today's trade volume is 1 million, with average price of $1.23, today's money flow is $1.23 million.

⇨ The total money flow is calculated by adding all the daily money flows together over the 14-day period.

⇨ The total positive money flow is calculated. The money flow is positive if the average price is higher than the previous day's average price. For example, if yesterday's average price was $1.19 and today's is $1.23, today's money flow is positive.

⇨ The total positive money flow for the previous 14 days is calculated by adding all the daily positive money flows together.

⇨ The MFI is calculated by dividing the total positive money flow by the total money flow and converting the ratio to a percentage by multiplying by 100.

The MFI can vary between extremes of 0 and 100 (percent). It will be zero if there are no positive days and it will be 100 if all days are positive.

Another way of calculating the MFI is to calculate the total negative money flow over the period in the same way as the positive money flow is calculated. Then the following formula can be applied:

$$MFI = 1 - 1 \div (1 + PMF \div NMF)$$

Where:
PMF = Total positive money flow
NMF = Total negative money flow

The MFI calculated using this formula is a decimal value so it needs to be multiplied by 100 to obtain a percentage. This method produces the same values for the MFI as the method I outlined because the total money flow equals PMF plus NMF.

Interpreting the money flow index

Like the RSI, the MFI can be used to indicate overbought and oversold levels and is interpreted in essentially the same way as the RSI. Like the RSI, it's charted as a separate chart below the price chart. The index tends to track in the same direction as price movements, so divergences between MFI trends and price trends can produce significant signals. As you can see by the way it's calculated, the MFI is a more sophisticated index than the RSI since it combines a number of prices and also includes volume. So you can think of the MFI as an index that amalgamates the RSI (modified) with OBV.

A great advantage of the MFI compared to the RSI is that it plays down the significance of price changes occurring on small volumes. As we've seen, low-volume price changes can be misleading because they often indicate price trend changes that end up being unsustainable. Therefore it's logical to conclude that, generally speaking, the MFI should be a more reliable indicator than the RSI.

Tip

I regard the MFI as more reliable than the RSI or momentum indicator for signalling when an uptrend is reaching the overbought level or when a downtrend is reaching the oversold level because it takes into account the positive or negative volume flow of money associated with the trend and not just prices. Also, unlike the RSI, it's not based on closing price only but an average of three prices: high, low and closing prices.

Overbought and oversold levels

With the RSI, default overbought and oversold levels are usually set at 70 and 30, although 80/20 and 60/40 are sometimes used. With the MFI, default overbought and oversold levels are usually set at 80 and 20. That's to say, when the index rises over 80 and remains above 80 for a number of periods it indicates that the shares are overbought and that a downward price correction is likely. Similarly, when the index tracks down under 20 and remains below 20 for a number of periods it indicates an oversold level and that an upward price correction is likely.

Example 1

Let's look at a price chart with the MFI shown. In figure 11.1 (overleaf) I've reproduced an OHLC chart with Bollinger bands, and below it the MFI chart. This chart is from the Incredible Charts site and is for Bradford Kendall (BKN) over a nine-month period.

On this chart I've marked four periods where the MFI exceeds the overbought/oversold levels, as follows:

1   The index indicates an oversold level is reached in the price downtrend. Sure enough, the price soon corrects upward. Note that price movement away from the lower Bollinger band confirms the move.

2   The index briefly reaches the overbought level before tracking below it again. Sure enough the uptrend ends and there's a downward correction, but it's only a brief one and the price tracks sideways for about a month. Again, the Bollinger bands confirm the change as the price bars move away from the upper band.

3   This is very similar to the situation at 2 in all respects.

4   The index indicates another oversold level, but this time the index signal is too rapid because the price continues to track upward and moves up from about $8.00 to $8.50 before the uptrend halts. Note that this time the Bollinger bands didn't confirm the MFI because the price bars didn't move away from the upper band but continued to hug it until after the price peaked.

Figure 11.1: OHLC chart with MFI

Source: IncredibleCharts.com

Tip

The MFI above 80 is a good indication of an overbought level and below 20 of an oversold level. However, these indications are not infallible; in an uptrend the indicator can remain in the overbought region for some time, and in a downtrend it can remain in the oversold level for some time.

MFI–price divergence signals

Divergences between the MFI trends and price trends often signal an imminent price trend change. These divergences can occur as follows:

⇨ Price trends up but the MFI doesn't follow suit and downtrends. This divergence signals that the price uptrend may not be sustainable because there's more negative money flow than positive.

⇨ Price trends down but the MFI doesn't follow suit and uptrends. This divergence signals that the price downtrend may not be sustainable because there's more positive money flow than negative.

⇨ Price sidetrends but the MFI doesn't follow suit and trends up or down. This divergence signals that the sidetrend may not be sustainable and could change to an uptrend or downtrend (depending upon the trend direction of the MFI).

Tip

MFI–price divergences are often reliable signals of an imminent price trend change. They're particularly powerful signals when they occur in the overbought/ oversold regions.

Example 2

I'll now revisit figure 11.1 to see if any divergence signals occur, and if they're reliable. Indeed, there are four that I've identified and marked in figure 11.2.

Figure 11.2: MFI divergences

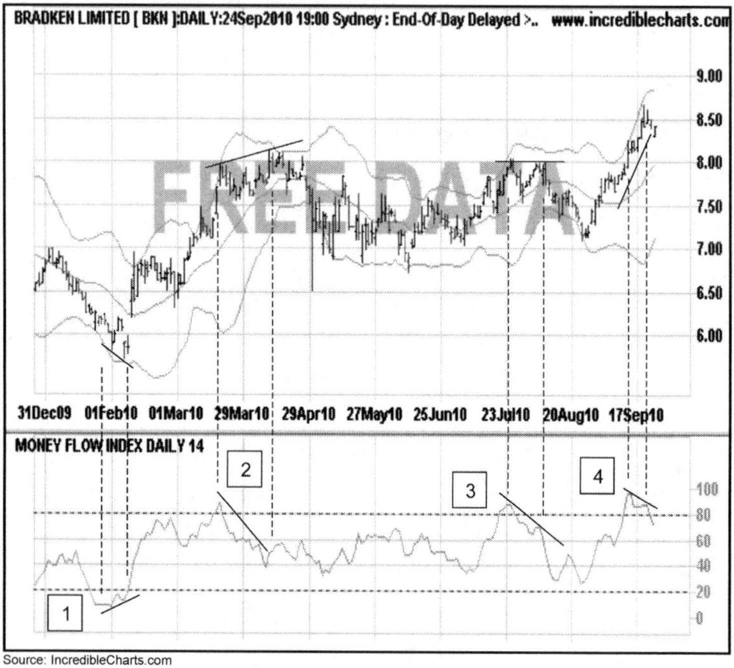

Source: IncredibleCharts.com

The divergences are as follows:

1   Price drops to the same or a new low but the MFI is rising. This signals a downtrend reversal. The signal is reliable because the price downtrend ends and a good uptrend commences with a price gap upward.

2   Price rises to the same or a new high but the MFI is falling. This signals the end of the uptrend. The signal is reliable because the uptrend falters, the price falls and a sidetrend wave is established.

3   Price double peaks to almost the same level ($8.00) but the MFI is trending down to lower levels. This isn't a true divergence because the price doesn't trend to quite the same high, but because the MFI is trending strongly downward it's a warning signal that's worth heeding. Indeed, the price soon drops to about $7.20 before an uptrend re-establishes.

4   Price rises strongly to a new high of around $8.60 but the MFI fails to follow suit. Sure enough, the price retracts from the high.

You can see that each divergence occurs at an overbought or oversold level, and is a reliable signal that confirms the overbought/oversold conditions in each case and is a precursor to a price trend change.

Chaikin money flow

The Chaikin money flow (CMF) indicator, named after its developer Marc Chaikin, is a rather similar indicator to the MFI but there are some significant differences. Unlike OBV and the MFI, positive or negative money flow isn't based on comparing today's prices with yesterday's (current period with the previous period). Instead, CMF uses today's prices only. The same three prices are used as in the MFI: high (H), low (L) and closing (C). A closing location value (CLV) is calculated using the following formula:

$$CLV = ((C - L) - (H - C)) \div (H - L)$$

In this formula, (H − L) is the price range.

Like the MFI, CMF can be based on daily or weekly frequencies. However, it's seldom used with weekly frequencies and I've assumed a daily frequency.

CMF uses a default time period of 21 days rather than the 14 days used for the MFI, and is sometimes displayed as a bar chart rather than a line chart.

Example 3

To show you how the CLV formula works, here's an example. Suppose that today's high price (H) is 80¢ and the low (L) is 74¢, making today's range 6¢ (H – L). The CLV for various closing prices is as shown in table 11.1.

Table 11.1: closing location value

Closing price C (¢)	(C – L) (¢)	(H – C) (¢)	CLV
80	6	0	1.00
79	5	1	0.67
78	4	2	0.33
77	3	3	0
76	2	4	–0.33
76	1	5	–0.67
74	0	6	–1.00

You can see that the closing location value can vary between –1.0 and +1.0, depending upon where the closing price lies in relation to the price range. If the closing price is mid-way between the high and low price the CLV is zero, if above the mid-point the CLV is positive and if below the CLV is negative. This is illustrated in figure 11.3.

Figure 11.3: CMF positive and negative regions

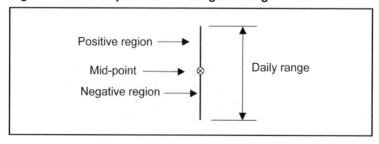

The closing location value for each day is multiplied by that day's volume to give a daily adjusted volume, which can be positive or negative. Adding the adjusted volumes together over the 21-day period gives a total adjusted volume, which again can be positive or negative depending upon the relative size of the positive and negative money flows over the period. Finally, the CMF is calculated by dividing the total adjusted volume by the cumulative total volume over the 21-day period to give a ratio that can also be positive or negative.

If the charting software as the facility, cumulative adjusted volumes can be charted—which shows a line known as the A/D line (accumulation/distribution line)—to provide a visual impression of the strength of the cumulative positive or negative money flows.

Interpreting Chaikin money flow

When interpreting the CMF chart (below the price chart), consider the following:

⇨ whether the indicator is positive or negative. A positive value is regarded as a generally bullish indication because it indicates buying pressure in the upper half of the daily price range, whereas a negative value is bearish (market weakness).

⇨ while the CLV can vary between extreme values of −1 and +1, CMF doesn't vary so greatly because it's calculated by multiplying the CLV by the volume and dividing by the total volume. So it rarely exceeds a range of −0.3 to +0.3

⇨ the value of the CMF gives an indication of the extent of the bullish or bearish sentiment. That's to say, CMF values of around ±0.1 are far less significant than those where the indicator reaches higher positive or negative values. The more extreme values of around ±0.3 are especially significant

⇨ the period of time in which the indicator remains in positive or negative territory. The longer the indicator remains in the positive region (above zero), the more consistent the bullish sentiment. That's to say, you can expect the indicator to remain in positive territory during an uptrend. Conversely, long negative periods indicate continuing negative or bearish sentiment and usually accompany downtrends

⇨ the trend of the indicator. An upward trending indicator indicates positive sentiment gathering momentum and is usually matched by a rising price trend. On the other hand, a downward trending indicator indicates negative sentiment gathering momentum and is usually matched by a falling price trend. As you might expect, if there's a large jump in volume (volume spike) the indicator will reflect this in a steep rise up or down (depending on whether the price change at the time is positive or negative)

⇨ indicator trend changes showing changing sentiment. If the indicator trends up and reaches a peak then starts to fall, this indicates a sentiment change from positive to negative and acts as a sell (or go short) signal. This signal is more definite if the indicator continues falling and crosses the zero line into negative territory. Conversely, a downtrending indicator that reaches a low and then starts to rise indicates a change from negative to positive sentiment and acts as a buy (go long) signal. This signal is more definite if the indicator continues rising and crosses the zero line into positive territory.

Tip

As a general rule, in price uptrends CMF will be positive and in downtrends negative. A change in trend is usually accompanied by a corresponding change in the CMF. However, these are general rules only and there are exceptions to them.

Example 3

I'll now look at a price chart in conjunction with a CMF chart to see if the indications I've outlined above are borne out in practice. Figure 11.4 is an OHLC chart from the Incredible Charts site for Bradford Kendall (BKN), including Bollinger bands and CMF, over a nine-month period.

Figure 11.4: OHLC chart with CMF

Source: IncredibleCharts.com

I've numbered the significant indications on the CMF chart:

1–2   CMF is negative but reaches a low at 1, then rises and crosses the zero line at 2, indicating a change in sentiment from negative to positive. This is confirmed by the price downtrend reversing to an uptrend.

2–3   CMF remains positive but is relatively low, indicating that the price uptrend isn't based on strong positive sentiment.

3–4   CMF turns down into the negative region and the price trends strongly down at the CMF low point.

4–5   CMF trends back up into positive territory but the price sidetrends.

5–6   CMF downtrends but the price remains locked in a sidetrend.

6–7   CMF trends up into positive territory and the positive sentiment is confirmed by a price breakout from a little over $7.00 to about $8.00.

7–8   CMF remains positive as price downtrends briefly, then rises to a new high of about $8.70.

CMF–price divergences

As you can see from figure 11.4, the CMF indications aren't always reliable. For example, between points 4 and 5 the CMF changes from negative to positive territory but this isn't matched by a corresponding price uptrend. Similarly, from point 5 to point 6 the CMF downtrends but isn't matched by a price downtrend; instead the price remains locked into what is essentially a sidetrend.

Often more reliable indications can be obtained from divergences between price trends and CMF trends. Divergences between the CMF trends and price trends are signals of an imminent price trend change. These divergences can occur as follows:

⇨ Price trends up but CMF doesn't follow suit and downtrends. This divergence signals that the price uptrend may not be sustainable because there's more negative money flow than positive.

⇨ Price trends down but the CMF doesn't follow suit and uptrends. This divergence signals that the price downtrend may not be sustainable because there's more positive money flow than negative.

⇨ Price sidetrends but the CMF doesn't follow suit and trends up or down. This divergence signals that the sidetrend may not be sustainable and could change to an uptrend or downtrend (depending upon the trend direction of the CMF).

Example 4

I'll now revisit figure 11.4 and mark up any divergences between CMF and price in figure 11.5.

Figure 11.5: divergences between CMF and price

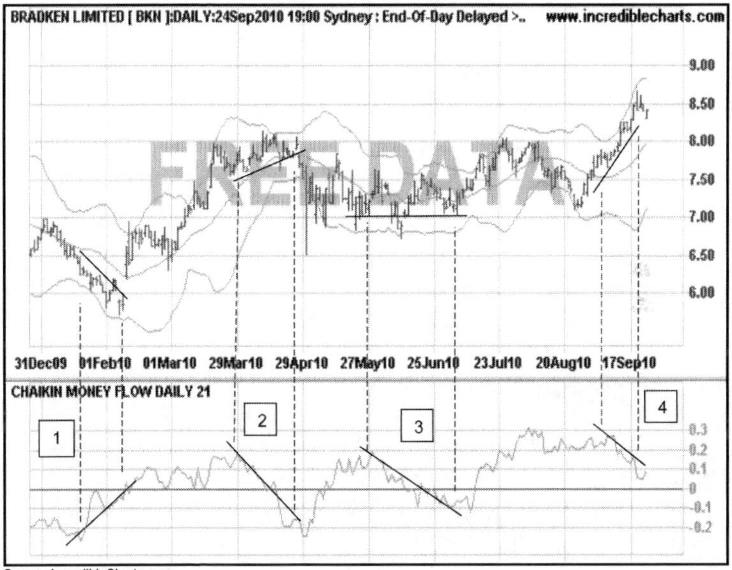

Source: IncredibleCharts.com

I've numbered the divergences as follows:

1. CMF trends up but price trends down. This divergence foreshadows the end of the downtrend, and indeed an uptrend soon follows

2. CMF trends strongly down into negative territory but price uptrends slightly. This divergence is a precursor to the price fall that follows

3. CMF downtrends into negative territory but price remains essentially sidetrending. This divergence turns out to be a false signal as the price doesn't enter a downtrend but soon rises. However, the indicator recovers and heads into positive territory, signalling a new uptrend

4   CMF downtrends but price strongly uptrends. This suggests that the uptrend may not be sustainable. Since we're at the end of the charting period, only the future will tell whether this divergence is a reliable indication.

Tip

CMF–price divergences are often more reliable signals than CMF trends alone. They are often precursors to a price trend change. The stronger the disparity between the price and CMF trend, the more powerful the signal. However, the divergence signals are not infallible and sometimes give trend change indications that don't eventuate.

Twiggs money flow

The Twiggs money flow (TMF) indicator was developed by Colin Twiggs, who's responsible for the Incredible Charts site (<www.incrediblecharts.com>). It was developed to overcome two basic flaws in CMF:

⇨   CMF is based on a 21-day time period. If a volume spike on a positive day occurs during the period, the index will jump up and reflect the spike. However, 21 days later data from the day of the spike will drop out of the index and the index will jump down. This downward jump can be totally misleading as it has no bearing on the price/volume action on the later day

⇨   CMF takes no account of gaps. Remember that CMF is based solely on the location of the closing price relative to the day's price bar. This is also misleading because if the price gaps up strongly but then closes below the mid-point of the daily price bar but still well above the previous day's price, the CMF will fall (even though the price has risen strongly).

In order to correct the first of these anomalies TMF uses exponential smoothing, so an early volume spike doesn't affect the index dramatically at the 21-day point. The second anomaly is rectified by basing TWF on the true price range rather than the daily price range. True range is a concept used in some other charting indicators (such as the DMI — directional movement indicator), and it considers not only today's price range but also today's high and low compared to yesterday's close. True range is defined as the largest of:

⇨ Today's high – Today's low

⇨ Today's high – Yesterday's close (on a price rise)

⇨ Yesterday's close – Today's low (on a price fall).

True range is more significant than today's range on occasions where today's range isn't very large but today's price bar is significantly above or below yesterday's bar. It's especially significant when price gaps occur as it will reflect these gaps.

Various scenarios where the true range (TR) is greater than today's range are illustrated in figure 11.6.

Figure 11.6: true range

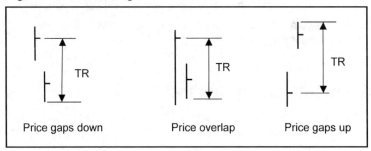

In this diagram for the sake of clarity I've omitted opening prices as they have no bearing on the true range. In the first diagram you can see that today there's a price fall but today's price range is smaller than the difference between yesterday's close and today's low. In the second diagram, today there's a price fall but today's low is well below yesterday's close so the true range is greater than today's range. In the third diagram, today the price gaps higher but today's price range is much less than the difference between today's high and yesterday's close.

Interpreting the Twiggs money flow indicator

You interpret the TWF indicator chart in exactly the same way as the CMF indicator chart, looking for positive and negative money flows, money flow trends and divergences between indicator trends and price trends. Because TWF eliminates two anomalies associated with the CMF it should provide more reliable indications, particularly where large volume spikes or price gaps occur. However, because it's a proprietary indicator it's not widely available with most charting software, though as you'd expect it's readily available on the Incredible Charts site.

Tip

The TMF indicator is very similar to the CMF indicator but can be expected to produce more reliable signals because it eliminates several anomalies associated with the CMF calculation. However, you're unlikely to find it included in any charting software other than the Incredible Charts site.

A flaw with money flow indices

Before concluding this chapter, I'd like to point out a flaw with all the money flow indices I've discussed. It's one that's not usually mentioned. All the indices compare one price to another to decide whether money flow is positive or negative. The MFI compares today's average price with yesterday's, and CMF and TMF compare the closing price to the mid-point price. But as I pointed out in chapter 9, significant price moves can occur on relatively small volumes and give a false impression. For example, suppose today there's been good buying support and the price rises strongly on high volumes. This exhausts buying support at the higher prices. Some low-volume sellers move in, and the price drops to below the mid-point price at close. The CMF will show the day as one with a high negative money flow (because of the high volume), even though the great majority of the trade volume was with buying support.

This flaw is, I believe, one of the reasons why money flow indicators don't always give reliable signals, particularly with the more speculative types of stocks.

Example 5

It's now time for you to have a go at interpreting a chart with an MFI. Figure 11.7 is taken from the Incredible Charts site and is an OHLC for Alumina Limited (AWC) over a six-month period. In this chart I've also shown a nine-day EMA for confirmation of the price trend. Below the price chart I've shown the MFI for the same period.

Figure 11.7: OHLC chart with MFI

Source: IncredibleCharts.com

Identify any trading signals from the overbought or oversold regions or divergences. My interpretation is given in appendix figure A11.7.

Chapter summary

⇨ Money flow indicators differ from other indicators such as momentum, RSI and OBV by combining price action with volume action in some way.

⇨ All money flow indicators can be based on daily or weekly frequencies, but daily frequencies are by far the most commonly used.

⇨ The MFI uses an average of the high, low and closing prices, and the money flow is calculated by multiplying the average price with the daily volume. The total volume is calculated over a past period that is conventionally set as 14 days.

⇨ The MFI can vary between values of 0 and 100. Values of 80 or higher indicate overbought levels with downward correction likely, whereas values of 20 or lower indicate oversold levels with upward correction likely.

⇨ Changes in direction of the MFI often accompany price trend change direction.

⇨ Divergences between the MFI and the price are often significant trading signals acting as precursors to a price trend change.

⇨ Chaikin money flow doesn't compare today's prices with yesterday's when distinguishing between positive and negative money flow. Instead it looks at where today's close lies relative to the mid-point between today's high and low prices. Above the mid-point is positive and below is negative.

⇨ The location of the closing price relative to the high, low and mid-point is used to calculate a closing location value that's multiplied by the volume to give today's money flow, which can be positive or negative.

⇨ The positive and negative money flows over a past period (conventionally 21 days) are added together and divided by the total (unadjusted) money flow to give the CMF.

⇨ CMF usually varies between –0.3 and +0.3. CMF is regarded as an indicator of sentiment; that is, positive high values align with positive or bullish sentiment and negative low values align with negative or bearish sentiment.

⇨ Changes in direction of the CMF line often accompany price trend change direction.

⇨ Divergences between the CMF and the price are often significant trading signals acting as precursors to a price trend change.

⇨ Twiggs money flow is a refinement of CMF designed to overcome two anomalies associated with the CMF, namely that CMF takes no account of gaps and that a volume spike on one day affects the CMF on a later day even though it's not relevant to the later day.

⇨ TWF can be interpreted in the same way as CMF and can be expected to give somewhat more reliable indications. However, it's not as widely available as the more commonly used CMF.

⇨ All money flow indicators are best used in conjunction with other technical analysis tools as they can give unreliable signals in some instances.

chapter 12

Your charting system

I've discussed only a few of the many charts and charting tools used for technical analysis; nevertheless, you're probably feeling a little overwhelmed and wondering how you can combine the tools and techniques into a coherent system. In this chapter I'll put it all together so you can develop a system that will work for you. Some of what I'll say is a synopsis of what's been included in earlier chapters; at appropriate points you may wish to refresh your understanding by referring back.

Creating a trading/investing plan

As discussed in chapter 1, you can buy or sell an investment instrument as a trader or an investor, depending on the intended time frame, the source of profits required and the type of instrument traded. You can also be a trader/investor or investor/trader if you allocate some of your capital to trading and some to investing. The important point is that, whether you're trading or investing, you should be following a plan.

I strongly recommend that you set out your plan in writing and that you do so before you trade.

Tip

Plan before you trade and set out your plan in writing.

Factors to consider in your plan

There are a number of factors you need to consider in your plan, including:

⇨ matching your trades and investments to your risk profile

⇨ your available capital

⇨ capital allocation

⇨ parcel sizes

⇨ share registration

⇨ your available time

⇨ profit targets

⇨ time periods

⇨ trading instruments

⇨ risk management

⇨ your trading method

⇨ choosing a charting site (or sites)

⇨ trading strategies

⇨ monitoring and reviewing

⇨ estate planning.

I'll now briefly discuss these factors. Because this book is about charting I'll concentrate primarily on the technical analysis aspects of your plan throughout this chapter. More information about investing plans is given in *Teach Yourself About Shares* (chapter 6) and *Online Investing on the Australian Sharemarket* (chapter 6). In addition, the latter contains sample trading plans for both speculative and defensive stocks in appendices A and B.

Matching your trades and investments to your risk profile

Generally, the greater the investment risk, the greater the potential return. The amount of risk you're prepared to take depends on your risk profile, so the first step in your planning is to determine your risk profile. A good way of doing this is by means of a risk profile quiz. Once you've determined your risk profile you're in a better position to match your risk profile to your investment risk.

Tip

The investment risk should align with your risk profile, so be aware of your risk profile. A risk profile quiz is included in Online Investing on the Australian Share-market *(chapter 6).*

Available capital

You need to decide how much capital you have available for investing or trading. It's not a good idea to bite into essential funds you need for your day-to-day living expenses, and you need to leave a margin of safety in case unexpected expenses arise. You may wish to consider extending your capital by means of a loan such as a margin loan. Gearing in this way or by other means has the potential to magnify profits but also to magnify losses.

Tip

Gearing your trading capital can increase your profits but can also increase losses if the market goes against you.

Capital allocation

Once you've determined the amount of capital you have available for trading or investing, plan how you will allocate the capital depending on whether you regard yourself as an investor, trader, trader/investor or investor/trader. If you're not an experienced trader it's best to initially allocate a small proportion of your capital to trading. You can start out in a small way and build up as time goes on and you gain more trading experience and confidence.

Tip

If you're new to trading, start out in a small way and build up as you gain experience and confidence.

Parcel size

Clearly the amount of capital you have available for trading has a significant bearing on the parcel size of your trades. You need to consider brokerage rates and fee structures because these affect economical parcel sizes. Because you can trade online with low brokerage you can economically trade small parcels and increase the parcel value as your confidence and success improves.

Tip

The lower the brokerage the smaller the parcel value you can economically trade.

Share registration

It's possible to set up share trading accounts for persons other than yourself, and if you trade using another account the shares will be registered in that name. Legally the account owner will own the shares and be accountable for the profits or losses and complying with taxation requirements. If you have a spouse or partner with a lower income than yours you can save tax by income splitting. You can also invest on behalf of a minor, but special considerations are involved.

Tip

Make sure you consider all the legal and taxation implications before you register shares in any name other than your own.

Available time

Trading, research, monitoring and reviewing takes time, and the amount of time needed depends on whether you're an active trader or a more passive investor. In your planning you need to consider the time you have available and that you can set aside for your trading and investing activities. Try to be realistic; for example, if you have a full-time job and you plan to trade on a part-time basis, when will you be able to do so? Will you really have the time or inclination to sit at your computer and concentrate after a hard day at work? Will sufficient time be available on weekends after you've fulfilled all your family and social obligations? Placing orders at times when the market is closed is fraught with danger so it's most advisable to trade only when the market is open, and this could be a problem if you're working at these times or involved in other activities.

Tip

Be realistic when planning the time you'll have available for trading and investing. It's usually not a good idea to place orders outside of trading hours.

Profit targets

You can trade or invest with the nebulous purpose of 'making as much profit as possible'. This is a statement of desire but can't be considered a profit target. Clearly set out exactly how much profit you intend to make on each trade or investment and whether your profit will be capital gains only or a mix of capital gains and dividends. You should express your profit target as a return on capital (on an equivalent annual basis). It's important to set realistic targets because if you set unrealistic ones you'll become discouraged if you fail to achieve them. Your profit targets don't need to be the same for all your planned trades or investments; indeed, they really shouldn't be. For example, if you're planning some short-term trades with speculative shares you would naturally set higher profit targets than for a long-term investment in blue-chip shares.

Tip

Set realistic profit targets; it's counterproductive to be overly confident or overly pessimistic.

Time period

Because your profit target should be stated in terms of equivalent return on capital, it's clearly necessary to plan the time period of your trade or investment. You need to decide whether you're investing for the longer term or whether you are aiming for short-term profits. Your planning should also consider what you'll do if you don't achieve the target profit within your planned time period—will you hang on for longer or will you close out the trade once your planned time period elapses?

Tip

Deciding on the time period of your trade or investment is a critical part of your profit planning. You should also be clear about what action you'll take if you don't achieve your target profit within the planned time period.

Trading instruments

Decide on the instruments you plan to trade or invest in. In this book I've considered shares only, but in the first chapter I outlined other types of trading instruments. If you plan to trade listed shares only you still need to decide whether you'll consider all of them or whether you'll restrict the field. If you are going to restrict the field you can do so by market cap or sector. For safer investing you may wish to consider only shares in the upper range of the market cap, such as those in the All Ords index (top 500) or more restrictedly those in the top 200, top 50 or even top 20. Generally speaking, higher market cap shares are less volatile and therefore less risky than lower market cap ones. For shorter term investing or trading you can consider restricting the field to a particular industry sector. For example, if the price of gold is on the rise you might want to consider trading some gold stocks for short- to medium-term profit.

Tip

Your choice of trading instruments should align with your risk profile, profit target and planned time period.

Risk management

Your planning should include consideration of possible contingencies and strategies for handling them when your trades don't go according to plan. The most likely contingencies you'll need to consider are that you won't achieve your target profit in the planned time period or that a trade will be showing a loss rather than a profit. Managing trading and investing risk is a large topic in its own right and in this chapter I can't possibly outline all the risks involved and strategies for dealing with them. In previous chapters I've discussed the particular risks and limitations associated with the various technical analysis tools and indicators and outlined strategies to maximise the upside possibilities with them while minimising the downside risk. You can obtain a more detailed outline of risk management in my other books that have whole chapters devoted to this aspect of trading and investing.

Tip

It's essential that your planning includes consideration of the risks involved and how you'll manage them. Consider placing stop loss orders so you can exit with minimum damage should the downside eventuate.

Trading method

Consider whether you'll trade online or offline and the types of orders you intend to place. If you plan to use conditional orders ensure that your broker accepts these types of orders and make the necessary arrangements with your broker. Brokerage on conditional orders will usually be higher than for plain vanilla-type orders.

Tip

Before you trade you should be thoroughly conversant with the fees and conditions associated with an order. If you intend to place conditional orders make sure your broker has the facility available.

Charting site (or sites)

If you trade online you should be able to access charts and technical analysis tools on your trading website. However, the site may not provide the charts in the form you want or provide all the tools and indicators you require. For technical analysis purposes you may need to consider using a charting site other than your trading site. If you're considering this option you'll need register and make any other arrangements necessary so that you can access the sites you want.

Tip

I strongly recommend that you access several sites for the purpose of technical analysis as the charting software and technical analysis tools and indicators can vary considerably.

Trading strategies

A vital part of your planning is consideration of the trading strategies you intend to use. This includes selection of the types of charting tools and indicators you'll use and the signals that will alert you to appropriate entry and exit points for your trades. Decide whether you'll trade in defined trends only (that is, be a trend trader) or whether you also intend to make profits by trading short-term price fluctuations.

Tip

The most consistent profits can be made by trend trading, but worthwhile profits can also be made in shorter time periods by trading the smaller price fluctuations that occur with day-to-day trading activity or with wave activity in sidetrend channels.

Monitoring and reviewing

Your plan needs to outline how you intend to monitor and review. This includes deciding on the frequency of your monitoring, the method you'll use and the records you'll keep. Please refer to any of my other books that have whole sections devoted to this aspect of trading and investing, including spreadsheets and formulas that you can use.

Tip

It's vital to monitor and review all your trades and investments on a regular basis and include the method you'll use in your plan.

Estate planning

Irrespective of your age or the condition of your health, it's prudent to include estate planning in your financial plan. None of us likes to dwell on the thought that we're not here forever but of course that's the reality and you need to consider estate planning. Strategies you're using now can have a big impact on your beneficiaries. For example, your beneficiaries can't write off any of your accumulated trading losses against future profits and the taxation benefits of them will be lost if you don't write them off while you can. Arranging your financial affairs to maximise the benefits for your beneficiaries can be a complex issue as there are legal and taxation aspects that need consideration. If you are at all unsure I suggest you research further and/or consult a financial adviser.

Tip

Ensure your trading/investing plan includes consideration of your beneficiaries. Include the relevant aspects of the plan in your will.

Putting the plan into operation

Even though you mightn't think so right now, developing a trading/investing plan is the easy part. The difficult part is putting the plan into operation because all kinds of contingencies can arise that tempt you to deviate from your plan. Human emotion often overrides rational considerations. If you allow emotion to influence your decisions then you won't be as successful as a trader or investor who sticks to a good plan through thick and thin.

Tip

The more dispassionate you are when making trading and investing decisions the more successful you'll be.

Technical analysis systems

As you can see, there are a large number of factors to consider in a trading/investing plan. A technical analysis system is a vital part of the plan, but it's more narrowly focused and is primarily concerned with charting and trading strategies based on chart analysis. I've illustrated this in figure 12.1.

Figure 12.1: technical analysis system and trading/investing plan

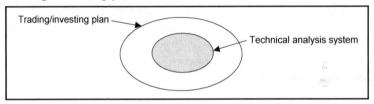

Tip

A technical analysis system is a vital part of a trading/investing plan but by itself it doesn't constitute a complete plan.

System complexity

As you've no doubt realised by now, technical analysis can be complex. In this book I've discussed only a handful of the main types of charts and indicators that have been developed over the years to use as tools in charting analysis. More than 50 different indicators have been developed and each is claimed by their developer to have superior features. Unfortunately there's little factual evidence to substantiate or contradict these claims, so in most cases you'll need to arrive at your own conclusions. I've attempted to provide some guidance when outlining the various tools and indicators by pointing out their advantages and limitations and the times when they might provide unreliable indications.

When considering the number of tools and indicators you'll use, the good news is that there's no evidence that a complex system using a large number of different tools produces better results than a simple system using only a few. Indeed, it's most likely the other way round, and after a certain point additional complexity can just muddy the waters rather than improving reliability.

Tip

You don't need a very sophisticated system with many indicators to have a good technical analysis system.

Success/failure rate

Given that no technical analysis system will always result in correct predictions, what's a good one? A good system is correct more often than it is incorrect. If your system has a successful prediction rate of 50%, rather than using technical analysis you'd be as well off basing your trading decisions on the toss of a coin. Mind you, as I demonstrate in *Teach Yourself About Shares* a successful prediction rate of only 50% (or even less) can still produce trading profits provided you're using a sound capital allocation and protection system. Naturally, the higher your success/failure rate, the more profit you'll make. For example, if you can lift your success rate by a small amount to just 60%, your success/failure rate will be 60/40 = 1.5, and that gives you an excellent opportunity to make good trading profits.

Tip

The higher the success/failure rate of your system the better it is and the more profit you'll make by using it. Even a small increase will give you a substantial trading edge.

Charts, indicators and parameters to include

I'll now outline some suggestions for the various charts, indicators, parameters and methods you can consider incorporating into your system.

Market charts

I suggest that the first chart you should look at is a market chart as this will give you an impression of market movements and trends. If the market is trending in a certain way it's likely that the vast majority of listed shares will be trending in the same way. This is expressed by the well-known saying 'a rising tide lifts all boats'.

A good way to gain an impression of Australian market trends and movements is to examine the chart of the All Ordinaries index (XAO) because this index reflects more than 98% of share investor dollars. Some sites, such as the Incredible Charts site, default to the All Ords index chart when you first access the site. If your charting site doesn't do so, call up the chart yourself.

Tip

Relative performance is often a more important consideration than absolute performance. Before looking at the chart of any shares you're interested in, examine a market chart to form an impression of the way the market is trending.

Price charts

After examining the market chart you can now analyse a price chart for any particular shares you're interested in. When calling up a price chart you need to consider the following variables:

⇨ time period

⇨ frequency

⇨ type of chart.

As discussed in chapter 2, these variables are interrelated; for example, candle charts aren't very suitable for long-term charting because the candles tend to merge and this makes interpretation difficult. Using a weekly frequency rather than a daily one makes interpretation easier but produces a much coarser plot. A line chart is the easiest chart to look at for the purpose of identifying longer term trends but it's not as suitable for shorter term trends because daily range data is omitted and gaps aren't shown.

For longer term investing, I suggest you look at a line chart over a relatively long term and then an OHLC chart or candle chart over the shorter term (six months or less). For the shorter term chart, the candlestick format with daily frequency is my preference as it's easier to interpret daily price changes from the body of the candle than from the small bars on an OHLC chart. For shorter term trading, you can omit the longer term chart as trends occurring some years ago will have little relevance.

Tip

Line charts best identify trends over the longer term whereas candle charts are better over the shorter term.

Other charts

Other charts you might want to consider include:

⇨ volume chart — to detect any volume trends or spikes

⇨ percent chart — for examining relative performance

⇨ equi-volume chart — for considering volumes in conjunction with price changes

⇨ point and figure chart — for confirming trends and trend changes.

Identifying trends and trend changes

Simple visual inspection of a price chart is often the best way of identifying trends and trend changes because there's less time lag than occurs with indicators based on historical price analysis. For example, consider the chart pattern shown in figure 12.2 (the wicks have been excluded from this diagram).

Figure 12.2: candle chart pattern

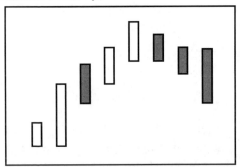

The three down-day candles in succession flash a warning that the uptrend has faltered. You're not able to tell if a longer term downtrend will follow or whether the change is just a temporary setback, but you're quickly alerted to the uptrend faltering. You can now examine the corresponding volume chart (or equi-volume chart) and check the volume on the down days. If the volume was substantial then alarm bells should be ringing. Trading movements early on the next day will give a better indication, and if the shares open lower and trade lower it's most likely that the uptrend has ended, so now would be a good time to exit (or go short).

Tip

Visual examination of a price chart is the most funda-mental tool you should use because it allows you to detect a trend change with minimum time lag. Consider volume in conjunction with price moves as volume affects the significance of the move.

Moving averages

After you've visually examined a price chart and framed your conclusions, next look at the chart with moving averages. Moving averages smooth out the day-to-day fluctuations and allow you to see trends more clearly. The downside is that a moving average is a lagging indicator, and the longer the term of the moving average the greater the time lag.

When calling up moving averages you need to decide on:

⇨ the type of moving average

⇨ how many moving averages to look at

⇨ the time period (term) of each moving average

⇨ the moving average signals you'll use.

There are basically three types of moving average: simple, exponential and weighted. I prefer to use a weighted or exponential one, especially with shorter term charts. A single moving average helps to confirm a trend and you can identify trading signals (golden or dead crosses) from price and moving average crossovers. Two moving averages with different terms allow you to simultaneously confirm both the longer and shorter term trends and also provide trading signals from their crossovers. Three or more moving averages provide a further tier of refinement, allowing you to use a very short term average as well as a medium and longer term one. The very short term moving average is equivalent to a line of best fit or trendline. There will be a greater number of crossovers and you need to decide which crossovers you will use as trading signals. Your decision depends on the amount of risk you're prepared to take and the planned time frame of your trade.

Tip

Moving averages are the most useful charting tool you can use, but remember that they're a lagging indicator. When selecting the crossovers you'll use as trading signals, table 5.7 in chapter 5 provides guidance.

Moving average convergence divergence

Visual trend examination in conjunction with one or more moving averages provides a sound platform for your technical analysis system. You may also want to incorporate other indicators to refine your analysis. In my opinion, the most important of these is moving average convergence divergence (MACD).

Unlike moving averages, MACD is shown as a separate chart below the main price chart. The charting software may show the indicator as a histogram or as two lines: the MACD line (fast line) and the signal line (slow line). If both options are available you can examine the MACD lines in conjunction with the histogram; this is my preferred choice.

Tip

The MACD is an excellent analysis tool to use in conjunction with moving averages. MACD crossovers are usually reliable indications of trend changes and have the added advantage that the signal generally appears with less time lag than moving average crossovers.

Bollinger bands

Bollinger bands in conjunction with a price chart provide very useful indications. In an uptrend prices tend to cluster around the upper band and in a downtrend around the lower band. Convergence or divergence of the bands gives an indication of volatility; the closer the bands, the lower the volatility. Bollinger bands also allow you to identify short-term trading opportunities that occur when price bars near an upper or lower band move away from it.

Another advantage of Bollinger bands is that they are shown on the main price chart and not as an additional chart below the main chart, so they don't detract from the available screen space. The only disadvantage is that if you're using moving averages the mid-band and moving average lines can mingle or cross over and make interpretation of the moving averages more difficult. Charts usually have different colours for the various lines, nevertheless in the interests of clarity I suggest you don't call up more than two moving averages in conjunction with Bollinger bands on the same chart.

Tip

Bollinger bands included on a price chart provide very useful indications and are well worth incorporating into your technical analysis system.

Filters

I've outlined the most useful primary tools you can use for charting analysis. It's often beneficial to look at some other indicators for confirmation of trend changes and trading signals. Additional indicators are known as filters because you don't use them as primary tools but rather to provide an additional tier of refinement. Many filters provide trading signals by identifying momentum effects that cause prices to reach overbought or oversold levels.

Indicators I've discussed that can be used as filters are:

⇨ momentum indicator

⇨ relative strength index (RSI)

⇨ on balance volume (OBV)

⇨ money flow index (MFI)

⇨ Chaikin money flow (CMF)

⇨ Twiggs money flow (TMF).

Which of these you use is a matter of personal choice but there's little point in using a number of them to provide essentially the same indication. For example, MFI, CMF and TMF provide basically the same indications but are based on different algorithms.

Tip

Don't try to use too many filters, and bear in mind that complexity isn't necessarily better than simplicity.

Divergences

Divergences between filter indications and primary trend indications from price charts and moving averages can provide trading signals. On the other hand, divergences can cast doubt on the primary signal. When a divergence appears you're faced with the dilemma of trying to decide whether the divergence is a trading signal or just an example of a conflicting indication. I've provided some guidance when I've discussed divergences but unfortunately it's not possible to state general rules that apply in all situations. That's a good reason to practise chart and indicator interpretation; you can become more adept at identifying divergences and deciding whether or not you should ignore them or use them as trading signals.

Tip

When prices move in a different way to the way you expected based on your technical analysis, it doesn't necessarily mean that your analysis was faulty. Markets sometimes jump in a manner that can be baffling to even the most skilled analyst and that's not predicted by any technical analysis system.

Optimising your screen display

If you have only one or two charts you want to examine you can call up a variety of different screens in succession. On the other hand, if you're like me you'll often want to look at 20 or more charts of interest. My core portfolio contains a fair number of different shares, and in addition to these I have a lesser number of short-term shares I'm trading or considering trading.

When you want to look at a large number of charts you need to maximise the amount of information in a single screen display. This avoids the laborious and time-consuming task of calling up a number of different screens and changing the parameters as you move from screen to screen. In addition to the main price chart, the charting software may allow you to display a number of different charts on a single screen, but if you call up too many the charts will be compressed and smaller so interpretation is more difficult. So you need to compromise between the number of charts displayed and clarity of interpretation.

For this reason, I call up only one or sometimes two additional charts below the main price chart. My first choice is the MACD and my second choice is the money flow index. Once I've set up the charting parameters I want to use, it's just a matter of changing the code to look at the next chart. To save time I have a list of codes I've compiled in advance so I don't fiddle about looking up codes while analysing charts. Using a single screen I'm able to examine a chart in 30 seconds or less, so I can look at 20 charts in 10 minutes or so.

After I've formed my initial impressions based on a preliminary examination of the single screen, I shortlist the shares that are candidates for trading or that require additional investigation. I then look at volume and some additional charts to provide confirmation or denial of my initial analysis. Finally, I examine an intra-day chart to check the most recent price action on the day I'm considering placing an order.

A time-saving feature of some websites (including the Incredible Charts site) is that they store the indicators and parameters you've set up and default to a screen containing them when you enter the site. This means you don't have to reset the screen each time you access the site.

Tip

Plan your screen to maximise the information you want without significant loss of clarity.

In figure 12.3 I've included a sample screen that I use most often for relatively short term trading purposes.

Figure 12.3: sample screen

Source: IncredibleCharts.com

It's from the Incredible Charts site and is a six-month chart for Bluescope Steel (BSL), and includes the following charts and indicators:

⇨ price chart in candlestick format

⇨ two exponential moving averages: 9 day and 25 day

⇨ Bollinger bands

⇨ MACD with histogram and fast/slow lines

⇨ money flow index.

You can see that the two moving averages and the mid Bollinger band tend to merge at times and they become difficult to discern. In the screen appearing on the computer different colours are used for the lines to improve clarity.

Shares list

I compile a list of shares (with ASX codes) that could be candidates for trading or investing from many sources, including:

⇨ newspaper articles

⇨ directors' trades (from newspapers or the internet)

⇨ magazines (for example, *Financial Review Smart Investor*)

⇨ financial institutions

⇨ broker suggestions

⇨ tips or advice from associates

⇨ website emails (for example, the Inside Trader website emails a trading suggestion each week)

⇨ online share forums and chat rooms

⇨ stock screens (discussed below).

Tip

The wider your information net the more trading possibilities will come to your attention, but never act on them without a thorough analysis using your system.

Stock screening facilities

Many charting websites provide a stock screening facility. The purpose of this is to use computing power to search for stocks that satisfy certain criteria you specify. With over 2000 ASX-listed stocks it's clearly very time-consuming to try to trawl through all of them to identify the ones that look interesting and present trading opportunities. Even if you did research them all, a week (or even a day) later the picture for many could be very different and you'd need to go through the whole exercise again. Using a stock screening facility it's possible to use computing power to search through all listed stocks or those listed in an index (such as the S&P/ASX 200, All Ords index or a sector index) and quickly obtain a shortlist of those that satisfy your criteria.

Stock screening is usually available on user-pay websites and is available free of charge on the Incredible Charts site. For example, you can screen for moving average buy signal crossovers (golden crosses). You specify the type of moving average, the time period of the shorter and longer term averages and the number of days that have elapsed since the crossover occurred. You could also screen for shares that have reached a new high or low in a specified time period, or if you're interested in longer term investing you could screen for shares based on PE or dividends. When you screen you can specify the search parameters: whether you want to consider shares included in an index or sector or whether you want to search the entire market. You can also specify the number of candidates you want included in the list.

The charting software will quickly provide a list of shares that satisfy your criteria. You can toggle between the list and your charting screen and quickly examine each chart to shortlist likely candidates.

Tip

If your charting software provides a stock screening facility it's well worth while using it to quickly obtain a list of shares that satisfy criteria you specify.

Charting records

When I'm investigating shares of interest for short-term trading I keep a record of my charting investigations. This provides a useful future reference and helps me to hone my technical analysis techniques as I can refer to the record and check my analysis at a later time. I use the KISS principle and jot down my conclusions in as short and simple a manner as possible. I use a single sheet of blank paper with ruled lines, but a computer table could be used for this purpose. The reason why I prefer a manually compiled table is that I can make notes as I'm examining the charting screen and I don't need to jump from one screen to another.

I record the date and examine each chart, jotting comments in the form of short notes such as:

⇨ potential purchase

⇨ sidetrend

⇨ downtrend

⇨ uptrend — too late

⇨ watch — trend change could be imminent

⇨ gap — check.

These notes have the following meanings:

⇨ *Potential purchase:* there's evidence of the early stages of a trend change, from downtrend or sidetrend to uptrend. This is the best time for purchase because there's greatest potential for upside profit. I also consider purchasing in an established uptrend if there are indications that there's significant upside potential remaining. I consider purchasing in a sidetrend if I can identify support and resistance levels (by visual examination or from Bollinger bands) and the price bars are close to the support level with indications of an imminent upward move.

⇨ *Sidetrend or downtrend:* these aren't of interest to me for purchase. However, if I think it might be worthwhile checking again in the future I make a note in my diary. For example, if I think the chart could be worth checking again in two weeks, I make a note to check it on this date.

⇨ *Uptrend—too late:* the price has risen strongly over the recent past and I feel it's too late for me to join the trend because there appears little upside potential remaining. In other words I feel I've 'missed the boat'. This is always a difficult decision to make; although riding an uptrend is the most reliable way of making trading profits, trends seldom continue forever, and joining a trend in the later stages when it's faltering (copycat trading) isn't a profitable exercise.

⇨ *Watch—trend change could be imminent:* this chart presents no features of immediate trading interest but there are indications that a trend change could be imminent. For example, there might be a sustained downtrend showing signs of faltering. It's too soon to consider purchase right now but if the downtrend definitely breaks these shares might be excellent ones to purchase in the future. When I think a trend change could be imminent, I make a note to follow up within a suitable time.

⇨ *Gap—check:* the chart shows a gap or gaps and I want to check any news or announcements around that time that could indicate a reason why.

After I've looked at all the shares in my list, for those that I've marked as having potential for purchase I change the screen and call up additional charts and indicators. If further investigation confirms that one or more could be worthwhile trading, I plan the trade in accordance with my system. After purchase I monitor the charts every day or two and examine them for another viewpoint; that is, to identify when the price is reaching my planned exit point. For example, if I'm trend trading I'll be looking for indications of a change in trend from uptrend to downtrend, and if I'm band trading and I've bought near the lower support band I'll be looking for a move back down from the upper resistance band.

Tip

It's well worth while keeping a charting record when you examine charts.

Chapter summary

⇨ You need a written trading/investing plan before you place orders. Your plan should consider a number of factors of importance.

⇨ It's essential to stick to your plan and not allow emotions to tempt you to deviate from it.

⇨ A technical analysis system is a vital part of a trading/ investing plan.

⇨ A technical analysis system doesn't need to be complex to be successful. Additional complexity doesn't necessarily improve reliability.

⇨ Before examining share price charts it's a good idea to examine a market chart and form an impression of market trends.

⇨ The price chart is the most basic and essential part of a technical analysis system. The line chart format is good for detecting longer term trends, and for shorter term trends candle or OHLC format are the most appropriate.

⇨ Charts such as equi-volume charts, percent charts and point and figure charts provide specific indications and can be worth viewing after you've examined a candle or OHLC price chart to help confirm or deny your initial impressions.

⇨ Moving averages are an excellent tool for confirming trends and trend changes indicated by your visual examination. However, there's always a time lag, and the longer the term of the moving average the greater the lag. An MACD chart can provide confirmation of moving average trading signals and do so with less time lag.

⇨ Bollinger bands are a useful inclusion on a price chart and don't require an additional chart since the bands appear in the price chart. However, the mid-band and one or more of the moving average lines may mingle and make discriminating between them more difficult.

⇨ You need to decide which filters (if any) you'll include in your technical analysis system. My first choice is the money flow index.

⇨ When you want to examine a large number of charts quickly you need to maximise the amount of information you can display on your screen. It's a matter of compromise because the more charts on the screen the smaller they'll be and the more difficult the interpretation.

⇨ The wider your information net, the more charts you'll need to examine. Never trade any suggestion (regardless of the source) before you conduct your own systematic analysis.

⇨ Screening stocks is very useful as it enables you to quickly obtain a shortlist of stocks that satisfy certain criteria you specify.

⇨ When you're examining charts to identify suitable candidates for trading, it's a good idea to record your charting investigations.

⇨ Your trading and investing profitability will depend more on strictly adhering to your exit strategies than on following your entry strategies.

Appendix
Chart interpretations

Figure A4.23: Lihir Gold (LHG) 6-month OHLC chart

Source: www.CommSec.com.au

I see this chart as a slight downtrend, followed by a break out to a slight uptrend. This uptrend could also have been interpreted as a double bottom. Then there's a big gap due to a takeover offer which took the price to a new high, after which a series of channels formed. I've also shown with dashed lines what you might interpret as inclined double bottoms and tops.

Figure A4.24: OZ Minerals (OZL) 6-month OHLC chart

Source: www.CommSec.com.au

I interpret this chart as a series of channels with a break out from each channel to the next. On close examination you'll notice that this chart contains a number of small gaps that don't seem to be particularly significant. There are also examples of wave action in each of the channels.

Figure A5.14: price and moving average crossovers

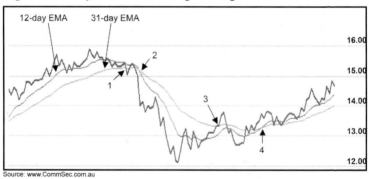

Source: www.CommSec.com.au

1   Warning — price crosses below 31-day EMA.

2   Dead cross — 12-day EMA crosses below 31-day EMA and downtrend follows.

3   Alert — price crosses above 31-day EMA (note that if you had used this as a buy signal you would have been whipsawed several times).

4   Golden cross — 12-day EMA crosses above the 31-day EMA and uptrend follows.

Figure A6.6: moving average and MACD crossovers

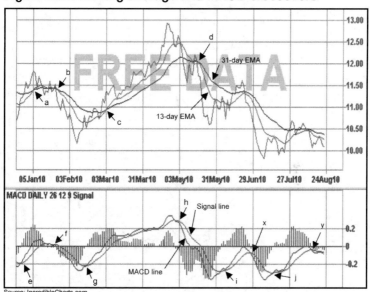

Source: IncredibleCharts.com

Moving average crossovers:

a   golden cross

b   dead cross

c   golden cross

d   dead cross.

MACD crossovers:

e   golden cross

f   dead cross (only just as very close to the zero line)

g   golden cross

h   dead cross

i   golden cross

j   golden cross

x   false dead cross (below zero)—but in this case a
     reliable signal

y   false dead cross (below zero).

Figure A7.4: OHLC chart with momentum

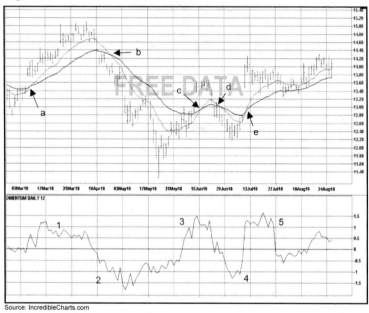

Source: IncredibleCharts.com

Moving average signals:

a   golden cross

b   dead cross

c   golden cross

d   dead cross

e   golden cross.

Note: signal c would result in a whipsaw trade if you acted
immediately.

Momentum signals:

1   sell

2   buy

3   sell

4   buy

5   sell.

Figure A8.7: candle chart with RSI

Source: IncredibleCharts.com

1   Double top divergence sell signal. Price reaches a new
    high but the RSI reaches the overbought region and
    turns down—a precursor of the downtrend that follows.

2   Buy signal as RSI reaches the oversold region and turns
    up as the price turns up.

3   Buy signal as the RSI reaches the oversold region and
    turns up as the price turns up.

4 Double bottom buy signal as the price bottoms again but the RSI is rising upward from the oversold region with the price—a precursor of the uptrend that follows.

5 RSI bounces down from the oversold region a number of times, providing warnings of an unsustainable uptrend.

Figure A10.8: OHLC chart with Bollinger bands

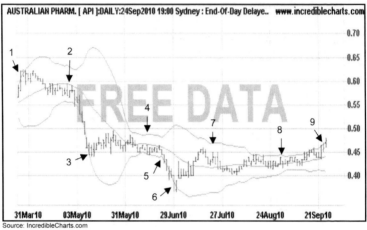

Source: IncredibleCharts.com

1 Uptrend ends, price bars briefly overlap upper band before moving down away from it (sell signal).

2 Trend change confirmation with mid-band changing direction.

3 Downtrend ends with prices moving away from the lower band (buy signal).

4 Narrowing band width and mid-band levelling indicates a sidetrend with low volatility.

5 Sidetrend changes to downtrend with price bars touching and overlapping the lower band as band width and volatility increase (sell signal).

6 Downtrend ends as price bars move away from the lower band (buy signal).

7   Mid-band levels out and band width narrows as a new sidetrend with low volatility establishes.

8   Very narrow band width confirming the low volatility sidetrend but mid-band starts to move slowly upward, indicating a gradual uptrend may be commencing.

9   Price bars touch top band and move upward, confirming the gradual uptrend.

Note: acting on the buy signal at 3 and the sell signal at 5 wouldn't have been a profitable trade but also not a disastrous one. Acting on the buy signal at 6 and holding to 9 and beyond is profitable.

Figure A11.7: OHLC chart with MFI

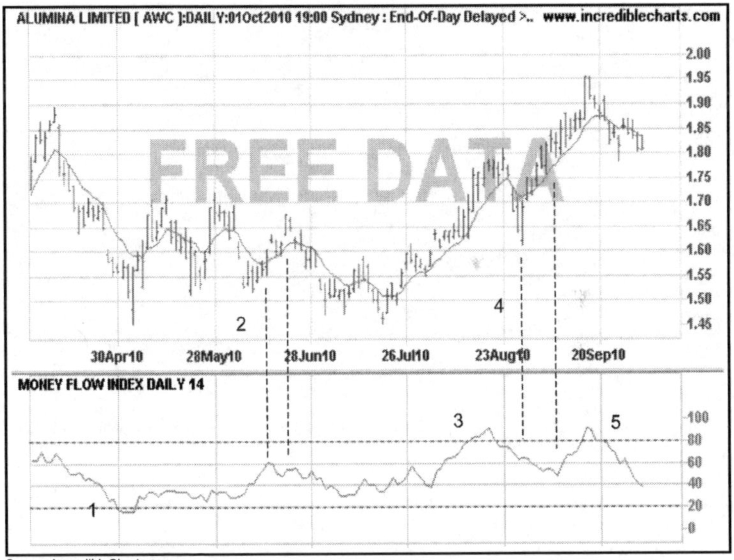

Source: IncredibleCharts.com

1   Buy signal as MFI enters the oversold region then rises. The price rises soon after.

2   Small divergence as price rises but MFI falls. This divergence is a precursor to the price fall that follows.

3   Sell signal as MFI exceeds the overbought level and is a precursor to the price fall that follows soon after.

4   A significant divergence as price continues to rise but MFI falls. This is a misleading divergence signal as price continues to rise.

5   Sell signal as MFI exceeds the overbought level and falls. This pre-empts the price fall that follows.

Note: the MFI trends in the generally the same direction as the price.

Index

Also in the Made Simple series

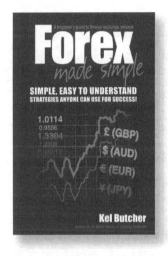

Available from all good bookshops

Printed in Australia
30 Aug 2019
716359